Spiritual

Recovery

Spiritual Recovery

A Twelve-Step Guide

GRANT R. SCHNARR

CHRYSALIS BOOKS

WEST CHESTER, PENNSYLVANIA

Library of Congress Cataloging-in-Publication Data
Schnarr, Grant R.
    Spiritual recovery : a twelve-step guide / Grant R. Schnarr.
        p. cm.
    Rev. ed. of: Unlocking your spiritual potential. c1990.
    Includes bibliographical references.
    ISBN 0-87785-379-7
    I. Spiritual lifeÑChristianity.   2. Twelve-step programs—Religious aspects—
Christianity.   3. Swedenborg, Emanuel, 1688–1772.   I. Schnarr, Grant R.   Unlocking
your spiritual potential.   II. Title.
BV4501.2.S2963 1998
248.4—dc21   97-44947
                                                                                      CIP

Edited by Mary Lou Bertucci
Designed by Eleanor Reagh, Big Fish, San Francisco, California
Typeset in Centaur by Sans Serif, Inc., Saline, MI
Printed in the United States of America

Chrysalis Books is an imprint of the Swedenborg Foundation, Inc.
For more information, contact:
Chrysalis Books
Swedenborg Foundation
320 North Church Street
West Chester, PA 19380
or
http://www.swedenborg.com.

To Cathy

Contents

Acknowledgments

THIS BOOK COULD NOT HAVE been written without the help of two great sources.

The first of these sources is the original twelve-step program used by Alcoholics Anonymous. These steps have been adapted with permission from A.A. World Services, Inc., in order to be of use for all people who desire to grow spiritually. The original twelve steps of Alcoholics Anonymous are as follows:

1. We admitted that we were powerless over alcohol—that our lives had become unmanageable.

2. Came to believe that a Power greater than ourselves could restore us to sanity.

3. Made a decision to turn our will and our lives over to the care of God *as we understood Him.*

4. Made a searching and fearless moral inventory of ourselves.

5. Admitted to God, to ourselves, and to another human being the exact nature of our wrongs.

6. Were entirely ready to have God remove all these defects of character.

7. Humbly asked Him to remove our shortcomings.

8. Made a list of all persons we had harmed and became willing to make amends to them all.

9. Made direct amends to such people wherever possible, except when to do so would injure them or others.

10. Continued to take personal inventory and when we were wrong promptly admitted it.

11. Sought through prayer and meditation to improve our conscious contact with God, *as we understood Him,* praying only

for knowledge of His will for us and the power to carry that out.

12. Having had a spiritual awakening as the result of these steps, we tried to carry this message to alcoholics, and to practice these principles in all our affairs.*

The second source of inspiration for this book is the work of the eighteenth-century scientist and theologian Emanuel Swedenborg. Swedenborg's books have been read and admired by such influential people as William James, Carl Jung, and Norman Vincent Peale. The similarities between Swedenborg's teachings about spirituality and those found in the twelve-step philosophy are astounding. Indeed, I was not surprised to learn that Bill Wilson, the author of the original twelve steps, was also familiar with Swedenborg's works and that his wife, Lois Burnham, the founder of Al-Anon, was a member of the New Church, a religious denomination founded on the Bible and Swedenborg's writings.

I also thank Rev. Michael Cowley for the initial concept of this new program, Peter Rhodes for some of the exercises at the end of each chapter, and Elizabeth Schnarr for reformatting the original manuscript into its updated form.

Finally, I express my love and respect for the special people whom I have met and come to know over the years in various twelve-step programs. I stand in awe of their honesty, courage, and desire to change their lives for the better. They have shown me through their stories that every person can become genuinely happy and spiritually rich, no matter what unfortunate circumstances he or she may have experienced.

---

*The Twelve Steps are reprinted with permission of Alcoholics Anonymous World Services, Inc. Permission to reprint and adapt the Twelve Steps does not mean that A. A. has reviewed or approved the contents of this publication nor that A. A. agrees with the views expressed herein. A. A. is a program of recovery from alcoholism *only*—the use of the Twelve Steps in connection with programs and activities which are patterned after A. A. but which address other problems, or in any other non-A. A. context, does not imply otherwise.

Additionally, although A. A. is a spiritual program, it is not a religious program. Hence, A. A. is not allied with any sect, denomination, or specific spiritual belief.

Introduction

[The angels said] that they picture wisdom . . . as a magnificent and highly ornate palace into which one mounts by twelve steps. No one arrives at even the first step, they said, except from the Lord by conjunction with him; . . . also as one ascends, one perceives that no man is wise from himself but from the Lord. . . . By the twelve steps into the palace of wisdom are meant good united to truth and truth united to good.

EMANUEL SWEDENBORG, *Divine Providence,* ¶36*

THE UNDERLYING PHILOSOPHY of the twelve steps has been in existence for a long time. Many different groups of people have used the steps to overcome their compulsions or character disorders. Alcoholics, drug addicts, overeaters, sex addicts, smokers, and gamblers use a form of the step program, as do those who have emotional disorders or are co-dependent. Twelve-step programs continue to spring up all around the country to help people deal with their specific needs and to find happy, healthier lives.

What makes these steps so useful to people to overcome their compulsions? Why have they proved so helpful to all kinds of people who choose to use them? Is it just a fluke that a couple of alcoholics banded together in order to stay sober and ended up creating some steps that can give every person who chooses to incorporate them into his or her life the ability not only to be freed from a particular addiction or compulsion but to find genuine happiness and spirituality? My answer to these questions is that it is certainly more than a fluke or coincidence.

---

*Emanuel Swedenborg, Angelic Wisdom concerning Divine Providence, tr. W. F. Wunsch, 2nd ed. (West Chester, Pennsylvania: Swedenborg Foundation, 1996). The number following the title of the work indicates a paragraph number, rather than a page number, as is standard in Swedenborg studies.

The underlying philosophy of the twelve steps has been in existence longer than most people know. Though these steps are said to have originated with the formation of Alcoholics Anonymous, the basic format contained in the twelve steps for achieving a happy, spiritual life is not exclusive to any self-help program. These steps—though called by other names, though sometimes condensed into more or fewer steps, though sometimes worded differently—have existed in many religions, philosophies, and psychologies throughout the ages. They are based on basic principles of our psychological and spiritual development.

Because these steps are based on basic psychological and spiritual truths, they work not only for the addictive-compulsive person but for all people who desire to grow spiritually. By applying these guidelines regularly and thoroughly, people have found and will find not only a new sense of freedom from the destructive tendencies within—from guilt, fear, anger, want, resentment, and others—but also a completely new way of life. Those who walk these steps find a happiness and a peace of mind they didn't even know existed. They undergo a spiritual awakening; they become aware of other people, themselves, their God in a new way that brings joy to their lives. They come into a new relationship with their God, one that is not based on blind faith and obedience but on an intelligent, loving, and free union with their Creator. They come into a life that can be truly called spiritual.

Those familiar with the twelve-step approach will readily understand the phrase "God as we understand him," as meaning that each person will have his or her own conception of God, and should feel free to fill in the concepts here with that personal picture. I have chosen to use the traditional AA approach in order to accommodate the vast number of people who are familiar with this phrasing. Also, my Judeo-Christian background refers to God in the masculine gender, a choice with which I am most comfortable in my spiritual quest. My Swedenborgian faith, interestingly enough, teaches me that God in essence is neither male nor female, but God came in person as Jesus Christ. I choose to honor this coming as it is explained in these familiar revelations. However, I urge the reader to insert his or her own conception of God in those places where I refer to a divine presence. There are many paths to the top of the mountain. I can describe only the one with which I am most familiar.

This book is a revised edition of an earlier work, *Unlocking Your Spiritual Potential: A Twelve Step Approach*, which sold more than ten thousand copies worldwide and has been used as a basis for support groups on five continents. The reason for a revision is that the original publication had all but one of the references to the teachings of Emanuel Swedenborg removed by the first publisher, who felt that not enough people knew about Swedenborg to market the book effectively. It was a sacrifice for me and a loss to the reader to remove such references because Swedenborg's writings not only provide a foundation for the twelve-step philosophy, but explain it on a spiritual level. I am delighted to have an opportunity to put out a new edition with clear references to and quotations from Swedenborg, for his works are my source of enlightenment on the subject.

Emanuel Swedenborg was an eighteenth-century scientist, philosopher, and theologian. His works put forth the premise that the spiritual path does not have to be enshrouded in a haze of mystery or followed by faith alone. Swedenborg posits that God created this world in a way that can be understood by every human being. All are welcome and able to travel the path to happiness and spiritual life; all can climb the necessary steps. Swedenborg's teachings have not only helped me to climb these steps but to understand how to take each step and why I must continue to move toward the top. This knowledge, in turn, has given me great comfort in accepting that there is a reason for every step on the path and a purpose behind everything I may encounter on the way. I know that these insights will do the same for you, as you follow your own path.

In the following chapters each of the twelve steps are discussed at length. I have tried to give not only practical advice on how to incorporate these steps into our lives, but also to explain why each step works and why we should follow them. I hope this book goes much deeper than other books into the underlying philosophy of the twelve-step program to give the reader a greater understanding of the reason for each step and for the program as a whole, the way it may be used in our lives, and the benefit following these steps may bring. In this way, those who desire may begin their own personal journey of spiritual growth with some understanding of where they are going, how to get there, and what they will find when they reach their goal.

The twelve steps for spiritual recovery have been adapted from the twelve steps of Alcoholics Anonymous.[*] In the following, I have italicized the phrasing that has been changed from the original AA step:

1. We admitted that we were powerless over our *destructive tendencies and that, when we followed them,* our lives became unmanageable.

2. Came to believe that a power greater than ourselves could *bring us true* sanity.

3. Made a decision to turn our will and our lives over to the care of God, as we understood him.

4. Made a searching and fearless moral inventory of ourselves.

5. Admitted to God, to ourselves, and to another human being the exact nature of our wrongs.

6. Became entirely ready to have God remove all these defects of character.

7. Humbly asked God to remove our shortcomings, *and began a new life.*

8. Made a list of all the persons we had harmed and became willing to make amends to all.

9. *Began to make amends, to do good, to be honest and faithful in all our affairs, and to walk humbly with our God.*

10. Continued to take personal inventory and when we were wrong promptly admitted it.

11. Sought through prayer and meditation to improve our conscious contact with God as we understood him, praying only

[*]Adapted with permission of A.A. World Services Inc., New York.

for knowledge of his will for us and the power to carry that out.

12. Having had a spiritual awakening as the result of these steps, we tried to carry this message to others and to practice these principles in all our affairs.

The twelve steps work. There is no doubt about that. The spiritual life is real, fulfilling, and attainable. Turn the page and begin your journey toward a new life. It is a journey with many hills and valleys, a journey with a few obstacles and pitfalls as well. But every step down that path is a step closer to the true meaning of life, a step closer to everything the more noble part of you wants to be.

Spiritual

Recovery

Step One

We admitted that we were powerless over our destructive ten-
dencies and that, when we followed them, our lives became un-
manageable.

FOR MANY PEOPLE WHO SUFFER from addictions and compul-
sions, the notion that a person can become powerless over his or her inner
destructive tendencies is a gospel truth. They have sensed the inner
bondage and loss of control. They have witnessed the destruction,
whether that be in their daily lives, within their family structure or work
environment, or in their own sense of human dignity and well-being. For
many who suffer from addiction, an emptiness within their core being exists, which seemingly cannot be filled. It is as if they do not have a soul.

The only time some people feel truly alive, at peace, one with themselves and the universe is when they feed that addiction in an attempt to
fill that inner void. Even though this "peace" lasts only for a brief moment, for a short time of chemical euphoria, of forgetting the emptiness,
and deadening the pain, that brief moment seems worth everything, de-
spite the ever-deepening sense of emptiness, loneliness, and desperation
that comes back after the fix has worn off. The addict begins to crave this
external means of achieving what he or she has come to regard as inner
peace and wholeness, regardless of how fleeting the feeling might be, or
how expensive the drug, or how much physical and emotional damage it
does. This is where the destruction begins, for those external means are
like sweet poisons that eventually kill. Whether it be alcohol, drugs,
gambling, lust, codependency, or the thousands of other addictions, the

effects are the same. Those who suffer from addiction cannot seem to live without their fix, and are driven to acts of desperation, pathology, and selfishness to keep it. All this, in turn, destroys their lives.

This is the reason that addicts immediately respond to the idea that they are powerless over these destructive tendencies. They know all too well what their destructive tendencies can do to them and all they love, and know how little power they have to deal with these tendencies on their own. But—and this may surprise anyone who has never suffered from addiction or compulsion—those in recovery confess their powerlessness with a smile and a sense of confidence, and even express joy in this knowledge. For recovering addicts to acknowledge powerlessness is to begin their spiritual journey and revive their inner soul. This confession marks not only the beginning of their passage to freedom but the awakening of their spirit. Through this first step, and the eleven that follow, they finally find something that truly fills the void that was their emotional life: a spiritual state of being that awakens, feeds, and even exhilarates their inner soul.

This new awakening can be experienced by all of us, but we need to take the first step of recognizing our own powerlessness. The idea of being powerless, however, is not easy for some of us to accept. Some of us who do not suffer from substance addiction may find it difficult to take this first step toward greater happiness and spiritual recovery. They may not understand that addiction is not the only type of destructive behavior that a person can display, not recognize that we all have the capacity to let our innate emotions control our lives. They may sense the inner void, the loneliness, the despair, and long for a deeper and more fulfilled life, but can't seem to get past this idea of powerlessness.

I can sympathize with this dilemma. When I first began to give public lectures on the benefits of these twelve steps to spiritual recovery for all people, a close associate of mine congratulated me on my efforts, but then confessed that she didn't think this program was right for her, explaining that she just didn't feel powerless. That saddened me; I had observed for years that my friend tended to be a controller and that she often fought hard to impose control on most aspects of her life, including her husband and her growing children. It saddened me because I saw that, until she realized that human control is an illusion and that her desire for control was hurting herself and others, she wouldn't grow in her peace of mind or in her trust in God and fellow human beings. It also occurred to me that, until she was willing to confront her behavior, she wouldn't see the bondage that it was placing her in. In truth, she was a very powerful person, but the power she exerted was not over her destructive tendencies. The power she relied on to control her world was actually destroying it, alienating those she loved, and creating fear and distrust in her own life. Until she could see this and accept her powerlessness over the destructive force within her, she wouldn't begin her healing and the awakening of her inner soul.

BEING POWERLESS

Are people powerless? Perhaps when we hear that suggestion, something inside rebels against it. Since we were young, we were taught to go forth and conquer the world, make a good life for ourselves, pursue a career, start a family, and become whatever we wanted to be. Many people do grow to become successful in business, marriage and family, in friendships, and to prosper. Certainly, all people have the capability to effect changes or make things happen in their lives, to build, change, mold, even create a life for themselves.

Still, we sometimes find ourselves powerless. Often, we set out to do something good or constructive, yet it ends up all wrong. There are those times when our own sense of power and desire to control seems to work against us and brings about an outcome we really didn't want. There are other times when we knowingly take an action that is hurtful to ourselves or others, but we can't seem to help ourselves. There is something within us over which we have very little, if any, power.

For example, John, a man in his late thirties, has been working hard to support his family, spending long hours at his job and taking business trips that keep him away from home many weekends. He finally takes a weekend off and hopes to spend some time with his young son Tony. Tony asks his father to teach him to play baseball, and John is delighted to have the opportunity. They eagerly grab the bat, the ball, a couple of gloves, and head out the door to reenact the World Series. But instead of creating quality time, John finds that it takes only two or three bad throws from Tony, a couple of empty swings of the bat, and a few missed catches until his impatience takes over. He hears it in his voice and sees it in his gestures as he tries to teach the boy the right way. Soon, like so many times before, John's voice breaks out into angry words: "I told you to keep your head up! Stand facing me! Don't be afraid of the ball! Stop crying! It wouldn't have hit you if you had been paying attention! What's the matter with you?" He watches in bewilderment as Tony drops the bat in tears and runs for home. John's heart breaks as he realizes what he has done to his son. He wanted to bond with his son, but his anger and impatience took over and destroyed what he had intended to be a valuable and enjoyable experience for the two of them.

In another instance, Judy, a young married woman, prepares a special dinner for herself and her husband to celebrate their second anniversary. She decorates the dining room, cooks a gourmet meal, sets the table with the special china, lights the candles, and brings out their favorite wine. Judy even left work early to get ready for the grand feast, which she has planned as a surprise to her husband Joel. But Joel doesn't come home at the usual time. In fact, he's forty-five minutes late. The meal overcooks, the candles burn a little too low, the wine grows stale. As Judy watches the clock and waits, she feels the muscles in her body begin to constrict and tension build in her chest. At first she wonders whether something is wrong; perhaps Joel has been involved in an accident. Then, as more time passes, and she sees the food and the whole surprise dinner spoiling, she feels a rush of anger mixed with fear. "What could have happened?" she thinks to herself. "He knew this was our anniversary!" After pacing back and forth by the kitchen window, peering out constantly for what seems like an eternity, she finally sees Joel's car pull into the driveway. He walks up the path and through the door; but, before he can explain, she lashes out at him with a fury. "Why didn't you call me? I thought something happened to you. I can't believe it! I prepared this special meal for us and now it's ruined! You knew it was our anniversary! How could you?" She storms off to sulk, still feeling very bad inside. Later, she comes out of her room to argue that he doesn't really care about their relationship or her feelings. Even after he explains that the traffic was terrible because of a bad accident and that he could not call her, she finds it hard to back down. Deep inside Judy knows that she overreacted, but she can't seem to help it. She feels all is lost now, regardless of the circumstances.

Think about that. Judy wanted to surprise Joel and have an enjoyable night together, but something else inside her rose up, took over, and actually snuffed out her hopes for an enjoyable time. What happened?

In another instance, Tom goes on a date with a woman he truly likes and wishes to know better. He has been through a lot of bad experiences trying to find a life-partner. Although he has no trouble getting dates, the women never seem to want to know him more deeply or have a serious relationship with him. On this particular date, Tom tries everything—the best restaurant, the most expensive meal, fabulous entertainment. But he recognizes two-thirds of the way through the evening that he is turning his date off. He realizes that he somehow manages to bend every topic of conversation toward himself and is trying too hard to impress her. On reflection, he realizes that this problem happens every time he takes someone out—self-centeredness takes over and ruins everything.

John, Judy, and Tom are not powerless to effect changes in their lives, but they are finding it difficult to control certain thoughts and feelings that bring them and those associated with them a great deal of pain. Although their intentions are good, a force rises up within them that destroys the very things they hope to accomplish. They are powerless over their destructive tendencies; they are powerless over themselves.

The controlling parent is another fitting example of destructive tendencies out of control. Perhaps you had or knew a mother who felt she had to control everything. The kids had to be completely clean, neat, and perfectly dressed every day for school. The house was immaculate and in order twenty-four hours a day. The dinner had to be out of the oven and on the table at exactly six o'clock every evening. The woman would become upset if her husband was late or a child lagged coming home from school. If something in the house broke down or one of the family members caused any type of disruption in the way things were meant to be, she couldn't cope with it and would leap in with all the zeal she could muster to bring things back under control. Everything had to be under control, including her husband's life and her children's futures. She was determined that, by her power, the whole family would live happily ever after. I think everybody knows someone like that. You can probably fill in the name of a relative or friend who fits this description; maybe you can even supply your own name.

What is wrong with this person? Because she believes she has the power to create and maintain her world, she carries that whole world on her shoulders. Although she does not realize it, she has turned her will and her life over to the destructive tendencies within herself. What is really controlling her world? It is her fears and her overwhelming concern for herself and her own sense of well-being. She has become so fearful of pain, rejection, and isolation that everyday she embarks on a neverending mission to protect herself by controlling every facet of her life. But she is trying to manage the unmanageable. No wonder her life becomes filled with dread as she runs to plug one hole after another in the imaginary dike she has built to keep pain out of her life.

There are various kinds of controllers like this woman. The sad thing is that life can look so peaceful and content on the outside but can be very disturbed, even chaotic on the inside. Sometimes a person can seem outwardly successful, seem to have it all, but may fail miserably on the inside. The soul is lost in a world of fear and dread.

Look at the businessman (or woman) who ambitiously begins his career with the complete certainty that he is the grand master of his destiny. He feels no need or desire to rely on a power greater than himself—he believes *he* is the power machine. Like a god, he will create his company out of nothing and run it his way to absolute success. And, indeed, working hard for years, he builds that company, buys his own building, and has a hundred employees working in ten different divisions.

But as the company grows, so does his burden because, after all, he's carrying that company. He's carrying that building and each one of those employees on his back. His desire for control rages out of control. He recognizes that he doesn't have to keep his hand in every single division to make sure things are working well; he could delegate responsibility to his workers. He realizes that he's being run ragged trying to be at every meeting or to close every sale. But when he takes a break from work, he has that terrible feeling he should be there. If the slightest problem develops, he feels anguish because it seems to confirm the notion that, if he had been there, the problem would not have happened. So he continues to work feverishly, controlling as much as possible to ensure success. Anything that he is unable to control haunts him. To the casual observer, he appears to be a perfect success, but inwardly he is failing. His business is under control, but life is unmanageable.

This man, like the previous example, is trying to do the impossible. Because he believes he has power and total responsibility over his world, he carries that world on his shoulders. He is no longer running that business. His destructive tendencies are running that business, the most powerful of which is his fear of failure.

Even more troubling are the cases of individuals who give over their entire lives to destructive tendencies, relinquishing their will and surrendering completely to their feelings of guilt. They are consumed in efforts to make up for past mistakes, trying to heal a festering wound. And there are people whose lives are dedicated to ego-satisfaction. They have to keep proving to themselves that they are special. They try to impress the most important person in their world, the one person who never seems to be satisfied with their efforts—themselves. There are people who are constantly running—from themselves, from reality, from responsibility, from hurt, from rejection. Outwardly all of these people may appear to be leading fairly normal lives, but inside life is increasingly uncontrollable; they do not know what happiness is. They are powerless over their destructive tendencies and have relinquished to these flaws all authority and control.

What do we have in common with these people? Everything. John and his impatience, Judy and her uncontrollable emotions, Tom and his narcissism, the mother and her rigidity, and the businessman and his ego are not strange people with some strange disease. We can understand every one of them because they are typical human beings like you and me. We all desire control, feel overwhelming fear or guilt, experience egotism, escapism, and low self-esteem. We all suffer from destructive tendencies at times, and the more we follow them the more they control our lives and make our lives unmanageable.

DESTRUCTIVE TENDENCIES

What are these destructive tendencies? Why do they exist and where do they come from? Where they come from must be left to the understanding of the individual, according to personal religious and philosophical beliefs or psychological analysis. Every religion has its own answer to these questions. Some say destructive tendencies are built within our nature; others suggest it is the devil working through us. Scientists tell us that these tendencies come from chemicals in our brain, while sociologists maintain that they are effects of our environment. I personally believe in a combination of philosophies for the origin of personal destructive tendencies. We tend toward destructive behavior because of a combination of heredity and environment, but there are also spiritual forces that influence us through these predilections and our own choices. Emanuel Swedenborg, whose theological writings form the basis of my own religious orientation, says that we are inclined toward destructive behaviors of every kind, but that we also have stored up within us many beautiful feelings and noble inclinations. Through our choices we determine which will predominate over our lives. Will we make our lives a miniature hell by following hellish influences that erupt in our destructive tendencies, or will we make our lives a miniature heaven by opening up to the positive forces of good that work through the more noble part of our being? The choice is ours, and it is a choice we make throughout our entire lives, in every new circumstance and resulting action.

When it comes to practical application, it doesn't matter that much if we can identify the origin of these tendencies. It matters much more that we acknowledge them and deal with them in an effective manner. Call them what you will—character defects, evils, neuroses, hang-ups—they exist within everyone from every race or creed. They are our fears, delusions, hatred, lusts, anger, contempt, foolishness, pride. They are real; they hurt. They are powerful and, when we follow them, they lead to pain, disillusionment, and, eventually, devastation.

THE LOWER SELF

The problem with believing that we are not powerless is that we tend to believe that we are all-powerful, and believing that we are all-powerful leads to believing that we are God. Instead of looking to any other source of love, wisdom, or happiness, we look for these blessings in ourselves. We believe we are the source of all we need. And that is simply not true. When we rely on ourselves for guidance and happiness, we shut the door to any higher or greater power outside ourselves. We give the seat of power over to the baser, more animalistic part within us, a decision that steers us on a course of misfortune.

These baser, lower qualities taken together comprise our lower self, the instinctive animal within us. The lower self is very much a part of us and, surprisingly enough, we need it. It contains our fears, our love for self, our desire for gratification; and these elements have their rightful place within us. Without fear, we wouldn't avoid danger; without self-love, we wouldn't protect ourselves; without a desire for gratification, we wouldn't eat or mate or provide for ourselves. We need this lower self, but it should *serve* us, not rule us. Therein lies the problem. When we reject any notion of a power greater than ourselves, we give the reins of authority to our lower self. It takes over and turns what should be constructive into something destructive. We begin to fear too much, to love self to the detriment of others, to take without thought of the outcome. This lower or natural self becomes like an animal that keeps eating until it dies as a consequence of its insatiable appetite. Instead of serving us, this baser self begins to rule us and to hurt us and others.

Thus, the lower self is bent on self-satisfaction; but, when it rules, it becomes a self-destructing force. How we judge the good in our lives is based not according to what might be best for us or others, or what might be best for us in the long run, but what feels good *now:* the quick fix, the false sense of security, the apparent love, the cheap thrill, and immediate self-gratification. In *Arcana Coelestia,* ¶210, Swedenborg bluntly describes this state of being, and his description is a wake-up call:

> *The human "own" [nature apart from God] consists of everything evil and false that gushes out of self-love and love of the world. It involves people believing not in the Lord or in the Word but in themselves, and their imagining that what they do not grasp through sensory evidence or through facts does not exist at all. They become as a consequence nothing but evil and falsity and so have a warped view of everything. Things that are evil they see as good . . . ; things that are false they see as true. . . . Realities they imagine to be nothing. . . . In the Word such people are called "the lame and the blind." This then is the human [condition], which in itself is hellish and condemned.**

We can see the lower self at work in the woman who dominates her family. She seeks a false sense of security by forcing her husband and children to act in a certain way so that she can feel good. She is not concerned for their welfare, although she probably doesn't recognize this fact. We can also see this with the man who loses patience with his young son while playing ball. He does not really think about what would be the most constructive way to behave with his child, but turns his life over to that lower, impatient, unloving self. That part of him does not even want to be playing ball with his son; it would rather be inside watching a ball-

*Emanuel Swedenborg, *Arcana Caelestia: Principally a Revelation of the Inner or Spiritual Meaning of Genesis and Exodus,* vol. I, tr. John Elliott (London: Swedenborg Society, 1983). All further quotations from *Arcana Coelestia* quoted in the text are from this edition. Another translation of this work is *Arcana Coelestia: The Heavenly Arcana contained in the Holy Scripture or Word of the Lord Unfolded, beginning with the Book of Genesis,* tr. J. Clowes, rvd. and ed. J. F. Potts, 2nd ed. (West Chester, Pennsylvania: Swedenborg Foundation, 1995–1998).

game on television and relaxing with a few beers. So the destructive tendencies come forth, and the father yells at and ridicules his child.

There are many examples of how this lower self operates in everyone's daily life. It encourages people to be underhanded in business dealings, to cheat or lie, while believing fully that this type of behavior will bring about greater success. It tells people that to hit back hard and fast when wronged is the best and most satisfying way to deal with others' shortcomings. It compels a man or woman to dominate the family in order to find fulfillment or the husband or wife to shout at the spouse before finding out the facts. It motivates the businessman to keep micromanaging his company.

We might say, "Big deal! What's the great harm?" But this same lower self causes people to hurt others not only verbally but physically. The lower self is responsible for all hurt and pain, for all cruelty and inhumanity. When it is not ruled by a higher power, it becomes impulsive, selfish, hateful. The lower self is not only responsible for impatience, laziness, indifference, and neglect, but also for every case of child abuse, assault and battery, rape, and murder. It is responsible for all the evils in the world.

LOSS OF CONTROL

How uncontrollable can life become for us? We can see that the more we follow the lower self and its destructive tendencies, the more outwardly unmanageable our circumstances can become. Even if we never commit a crime or do anything society may call immoral, we may still suffer from an unmanageable inner life. We can gain the whole world by following these tendencies but lose our own soul because inside we feel empty, lost, spiritually bankrupt, and devastated. The lower self is never happy with life as it is. If we search for happiness through our destructive tendencies, we often lose the very thing we wanted in the first place. Instead of finding happiness, we know only frustration. Instead of fulfillment, we suffer from hunger and want. Instead of peace of mind or security, we end up trapped in our own fears. These baser feelings always lead away from our true goal.

Let us return to the woman who wants to control everything. She desires a good marriage and a good family. Fair enough. But what does she do to fulfill this desire? Since she has turned over control to the destructive tendencies within her—her fears and self-centeredness—she tries to create the perfect family through manipulation. Through both subtle and not-so-subtle means, she makes sure her husband acts the way she wants and her children fulfill their mother's dreams for them. And she ends up with children who, when they are around Mom, act the way Mom wants them to and with a husband who *seems* to be perfect. But they are puppets. They act this way because they are afraid not to or would rather avoid than confront the consequences of their disappointing the woman's expectations. Moreover, the woman herself is not happy. Outwardly, she seems to have what she wanted; but, in her heart, she knows that something is missing. She certainly can't control the part that is inside of her husband and children—how her family thinks and feels about her. And this drives her crazy. She feels unloved and inwardly rejected by her family, yet she can do nothing about it. Her destructive tendencies have made her worst fears come true.

Look at the motivation of the businessman. His fear of failure forces him figuratively to harness the company to his back and leads him to keep his hand in every branch of the business. He can build the company into a highly successful corporation and virtually kill himself trying to control it, but he will never be happy. Fear of failure does not know the meaning of happiness or contentment. It is a destructive inclination that is never satisfied. Without a higher power leading him in a different direction, the businessman is doomed to serve this fear, although, to others, he appears to be the "boss."

We may not turn into monsters when, for instance, our impatience or anger breaks out at our children or spouse, but what prevents us from being impatient or angry for the rest of our lives? Nothing. In fact, we get worse and make ourselves and everyone around us more unhappy. We can live what seem to be normal lives on the outside; but, without a higher power guiding us away from the control of those destructive tendencies, our lives become a confused and frustrating existence on the inside.

HITTING BOTTOM

In order to achieve real happiness and a spiritual life, we must come to see that our lives become unmanageable when we rely on ourselves alone. We have to "hit bottom." For an alcoholic, "hitting bottom" is recognizing that he or she is powerless over alcohol and must get help to overcome the addiction. Some people have "higher bottoms" than others (and this has nothing to do with their physique). Some people see the writing on the wall when they miss their first day of work because of a hangover or when they almost demolish the car while under the influence. They are the lucky ones. Others have to lose their jobs or kill someone in a car accident before they realize how out of control their lives have become.

When it comes to our spiritual lives, we must also hit bottom. We must come to see the hurt we can cause ourselves and others when we follow our destructive tendencies. We, like the alcoholic or compulsive person, must see that, left to ourselves, we are powerless over our baser instincts. The more we allow them to drive us the more unmanageable life becomes, both within and without.

But the wonderful thing is that we do not have to let these tendencies destroy us before coming to this realization. We can hit bottom in our imagination. Without actually doing certain destructive actions, we can see what the consequences will be. We do not have to injure someone to know cruelty. We do not have to go on wild sexual escapades to know lust. We do not have to steal to know covetousness. We do not have to lie to know deceit. We can know all those things without acting them out and can recognize our powerlessness over baser desires without having to experience that powerlessness in some catastrophic way.

We can hit bottom spiritually before we crash to the bottom in our natural lives—and come to see that only a power greater than ourselves can bring true sanity and order to our lives. When we come to this recognition, we then stop running the show and begin to allow a power greater than ourselves to help us. We say, "O.K. God, or whoever you are, I lost the game when I played on my own. It's your turn now." Amazingly enough, when we say such a sentiment from the heart, a higher power does move into action and begin to order our life and helps us win the game.

When we admit we are powerless over our destructive tendencies, we begin to glimpse another reality; and, for the first time, that persuasive invasion of the lower self is stopped. For the first time, we begin to feel real or genuine control over our lives. For the first time, we feel a warm and loving presence—our higher power—that comforts us and gives us peace. As Swedenborg states in *Arcana Coelestia*, ¶2694, "[T]hose who are being reformed are brought into a state of . . . grief and despair . . . [and] for the first time receive comfort and help from the Lord. . . ."

When we finally hit bottom and admit that we need a higher power, God, as we understand God, can begin to work within us because now we are inviting God in. We open a door and allow the Divine to enter us, take charge, and move us in the right direction. No longer do we listen to and blindly follow those destructive voices inside. We have confessed that they will lead us nowhere but down. We recognize with the heart, perhaps for the first time in our lives, that we are not God. We are not all-powerful. In fact, we have no power without the Divine, as our destructive tendencies have proved. When we come to this recognition, we are ready to move forward toward a true spiritual life. We leave the slavery of those destructive tendencies and head toward the promised land of spirituality, a land of happiness and fulfilled dreams. We are ready for true sanity, happiness, and spiritual life.

EXERCISES FOR STEP ONE

Becoming aware of our powerlessness and our lower selves

1. Reflect on the troubled areas in your life. To what degree do you have power to change these for the better? Write down the areas you recognize and have tried to change but seem powerless to do so.

2. When you become aware of a destructive emotion, notice what thoughts come with it and how quickly they arrive. When a destructive emotion arises, experiment with stopping the thought. Notice changes in the emotions.

Step Two

Came to believe that a power greater than ourselves could bring us true sanity

STEP TWO SUGGESTS THAT, prior to this time, we may not have been sane. In fact, it implies that in the past we were insane. For some, this is hard to believe. But the second step also leads to some very positive changes in our character. By means of a higher power we can be brought not only to true sanity but also to genuine happiness and a spiritual life. If you are bothered by the notion that you may not always have been completely sane, keep reading and keep an open mind. Once we define the problems, we can define the solutions.

SPIRITUAL INSANITY

Is it true that not only are we powerless at times but also insane? Yes. We can be, but we do not have to be. Let's explore what we mean by the word "insanity."

A dictionary definition of the word *insanity* describes it as a state of serious mental disorder or derangement. Often such insane individuals cannot even take care of themselves. But step two is not talking about this type of insanity. People who suffer from "clinical insanity" clearly suffer from a problem that is beyond their freedom and control. Step two refers to a type of insanity that people freely bring upon themselves.

We come closer to the type of insanity when we explore the legal definition of insanity. Generally, the word "insanity" is used in a court-room to mean the inability to know the difference between right and wrong. If a person is mentally incompetent and consequently cannot know the difference between right and wrong, then that person is not held responsible for his or her actions. This inability to see the difference be-tween right and wrong is closer to the definition of insanity we are speak-ing of, but it is still not exact. Both the legal definition and the standard dictionary definition of insanity exclude one element that separates them from the insanity spoken of in step two. That ingredient is *freedom*. Those who suffer from clinical or legal insanity aren't completely free to choose their behavior. The insanity we are talking about here is a type of mental derangement that people freely bring upon themselves. It is not an inabil-ity to know the difference between right and wrong but an unwillingness to recognize that difference.

When someone does something wrong and does not know that it is wrong, we generally recognize that the person cannot be held responsible for the action. No one can be held justly accountable for doing something in complete ignorance, if he or she lacks the ability to correct that igno-rance. But what about a person who *does* know the difference between right and wrong and chooses the wrong anyway? Worse yet, what if the person knows the difference between right and wrong but *chooses to forget* that difference? What if a person destroys his or her life by making free choices to think and do things that stand in the way of the true goals that person wanted to achieve? That would be insane. Indeed, that is spiritual insanity.

Spiritual insanity is knowing what is right, is hearing what is right, but doing the opposite anyway. In its purest definition, spiritual insanity is an aversion to or rejection of the truth. It is freely choosing to believe and follow something false over what is true. In *True Christian Religion*, ¶589, Swedenborg describes people who have purposely chosen to live in mili-tant denial:

> Such are not intelligent but insane in spiritual things, because they do not will good but evil; consequently, they are averse to knowing and understanding truth, for truth

*favors good and opposes evil. . . . [T]he first step in the new birth is a reception of truth by the understanding, and the second is the will to act in accordance with truth, and finally to practice it.**

In this book, I define "truth" as the essential reality that leads to good. If an action or thought leads to goodness, order, happiness, and love, then it is true. What I call truth here is what most religions call truth: the basic laws of civility, love, and morality that lead to a happy life and a better relationship with our God.

You can see, then, why it is insane to hold an inward aversion to truth. Simply put, if truth is reality and we are adverse to reality, then we are spiritually insane.

Unfortunately, so often people turn away from what they know in their hearts to be true. People can see, if they want to, that loving others really is a beautiful emotion that leads to a happier, more fulfilling life for all. It makes sense, and it feels right. Nevertheless, people often find themselves controlled by the lower, more animalistic self, which entices, nudges, pushes, and shoves them to go against what they know is true. The most persuasive thoughts convince them that love is a joke, that other people are adversaries to be fought. Often enough people reject the truth about charity and turn to combat instead.

As is commonly said in twelve-step groups, "Denial ain't just a river in Egypt." Everyone suffers from denial. The more people act from their lower self the more prone they are to make up excuses for not choosing what they know is the best option. After deceiving themselves for a time, people can end up fully believing those excuses, denials, and false ideas, even to hold them to be the absolute truth. They believe with all their hearts that those false ideas will lead to goodness and happiness. Caught in a mental trap, they experience ever-increasing

*Emanuel Swedenborg, *True Christian Religion*, 2 vols., tr. J. C. Ager, 2nd ed. (West Chester, Pennsylvania: Swedenborg Foundation, 1996). All further quotations from *True Christian Religion* are from this source and will be cited in the text.

unhappiness and chaos, but still believe that they are on the right track and that happiness and fulfillment are right around the corner. Thus, their insanity is a very real mental affliction. They are not only averse to the truth but embrace what is false. In the end, what is false they call true and what is destructive or evil they call good. When people begin thinking like this, they become spiritually insane and head toward self-induced unhappiness and unmanageability

ALTERNATIVE PATHS

Imagine that we are standing before a great mountain. At the top of that mountain is happiness, fulfillment, success in life, heaven, whatever else we desire. Each of us has been given a map and a set of directions. For some, this map is the Bible, the Koran, or any other text held to be inspired; for others, it is other personal revelations. For some, it is what they have learned from mentors or experience. I prefer to use the Bible and the teachings of Emanuel Swedenborg to help me to understand the Bible. This is my map and these are my directions, but there are many maps, just as there are paths, that lead to the top of the mountain.

Whatever guide we follow, this map is the truth each of us knows and accepts about life. Each map provides a set of guidelines, whether in commandments or rules for living, that are designed to lead us to our true goal, a good life on this earth and unity with God. Let's depict that goal as the top of the mountain and translate those various directions into something like this: "If you look up, there is a small crevice straight ahead of you. It is narrow but you can get through. Climb straight up through it. It may seem a bit difficult, but, once you get through this crevice, there are just a few more modest slopes and then you will be at the top. This is not only the best, but the safest way to get to the top of the mountain."

No problem so far. You understand the directions and take a look up-ward to scan the situation. It occurs to you that these instructions won't provide a particularly easy or even interesting climb. You look around for possible alternatives and are struck by a very tempting one to your left. You glance down at your map to see if it sheds any light on this particular path and are surprised to read an annotation to this path: "Don't take this path! If you look over to your left, there is what appears to be a path on top of a snowbank. It looks as though you could walk ten or fifteen feet up the path and be at the top of the mountain, but it is an illusion. If you walk out onto that snowbank, it will collapse, and you will fall twenty to thirty feet and break your leg. You might even kill yourself!" (Some versions of our maps may say, "Thou shalt not take the left route or thou shalt surely be smitten.")

When you allow the lower self to direct you, what do you so often do in this situation? Since the lower self hates following directions and tends to take over in times like these, under its influence, you probably re-examine your map. You look at the prescribed way in front of you, a hard climb as far as you can see, and gaze longingly at the snowbank that looks safe and easy. So, you go trotting out onto the snowbank. Ten feet to heaven! Nine! Eight! All of a sudden the snowbank collapses under your feet. You fall, as the directions said, and break an ankle.

Is that insane? No, that's not insane; that's merely human nature. Everyone tests things once. It is insane when you get up on one leg, hop back up on the path, looking at both routes, and take the snowbank path again, perhaps taking a bit more care this time. Of course, you fall a second time, only this time you break a leg. You go further into insanity when you crawl back up the hill and take the same route again, and then again, each time saying, "This time it's going to work." But it doesn't. That's spiritual insanity.

As a counselor, I have met countless people who exhibit this behavior. For example, many people are looking for love and a sense of unity with another person, but keep taking an alternate path of casual sexual relations to try to get there. Instead of achieving love, they end up in a superficial relationship. They use their temporary partner to get a quick, yet not very satisfying, sense of togetherness, mixed with a cheap thrill. They want love and togetherness, but, through selfish sexual relationships, they burn out the potential for these things with that particular partner. When this develops into a continual pattern, it is called sexual addiction.

I knew a young girl who had a lot of problems with her family life, especially her relationship with her father. She desperately wanted to love and be loved, and she really needed to touch·people, to be close, to feel warm and loved. It was sad because, when she came into puberty, she jumped into the playground of sexual experience and proceeded on all sorts of different sexual excursions looking for love. She wanted warmth and love, but it didn't take her long after some very bad experiences to conclude that there is no such thing as love, that "men stink," and that life, at least at that time, had nothing of value to offer her.

Many people keep trotting out on that alternate route looking for love. Their dreams for a life-partner keep collapsing under their feet, and they hit bottom again and again with each relationship. They will keep falling until they compel themselves to go another way. They must come to see that lust and love don't mix. If they want to get to the top of the mountain, they have to let their relationships build within before they come together without. Their minds must fall in love before their bodies fall into bed. They have to take the long road of commitment and mutual support. This route may not appear exciting, but, when they begin to walk this path, they recognize that this way is better—the way that brings the warmth and love they desire. Even the physical act of sex itself becomes more delightful with a new attitude of commitment and giving. In his work on love in marriage, Swedenborg says that love based on commitment and sharing leads to more happiness than can be imagined, but he calls the highs of self-satisfying sexual addiction, "the pleasures of insanity" (*Conjugial Love*, ❡ 423).

HITTING THE WALL

Let's consider another illustration for this type of spiritual insanity. Imagine we are standing in front of a large wall; happiness is on the other side of the wall. Once again, we get a set of directions that tells us how to get to the other side. We are told, "Through this little, unadorned door is a place of indescribable beauty. Through this door lies happiness, joy, peace, and contentment. Open this door. But beware: any other door you might see along this wall is an illusion, a lie and a fantasy."

So we stand there, look at the wall, and see the door. It doesn't really look too inviting. Perhaps we'll open it some day, but, for now, we'll just look around for other alternatives. Sure enough, other alternatives do arise; other doors begin to appear on the wall. They are nothing like the plain door we've been told to go through. These are magnificent! As we peer through these doors, we see all sorts of interesting things happening. Behind some, people are counting money, holding up bags of it, and calling out for us to take them. Behind others, we see servants waiting to obey our every command. Behind still others we see people laughing and partying together without a responsibility or care in the world. There are hundreds of other doors. All of them reveal different enticing scenes that appear to lead to the other side.

We know what we do when our lower self is in charge. We bolt for the door that opens into our fantasy. But as soon as we reach the door, what happens? It disappears, and with a thud we hit the wall. After all, it is an illusion. Don't forget: on the other side of the wall lies happiness. The scenes that appeared to be on the other side of the wall were only fantasies of happiness. Those doors don't lead to the other side; but, when we are acting from our lower self, we keep trying them. We keep running full force into those different illusions until we are bruised and bloodied. Sometimes we recognize the pain we cause ourselves and think twice before we try the same door again, but a slightly different door always seems to open up to us. We leap at it believing that this time the fantasy might be real and we just might end up on the other side.

Can you imagine walking down the street and seeing someone running into a wall over and over again? Would you think the person insane? Of course. But in our spiritual lives, when ruled by the lower self, we do that sort of thing all the time. We are told that if we love, we will be loved. Yet, when ruled by the lower self, we hate. Give, we've been told, and you will receive. Instead, we take. We don't want people to reject us, but often we reject them before they can reject us. We want to share warmth, love, and companionship with others; but we build walls around ourselves so people can't get in and perhaps hurt us. Often, when we let our lower self seize control, we go against what we know will bring true happiness.

One example of hitting the wall is marital infidelity. How many married people have experienced the illusion that they will find happiness in an affair? Perhaps they have grown tired of their partner's treating them badly or ignoring them, tired of the low self-esteem they feel in their marriage relationship. Then someone comes along who shows an interest in them. The illusory door to happiness suddenly appears. If they follow their destructive feelings, they pursue the new prospect and have an affair. I have yet to meet anyone who has made it through the wall. They hit it hard. Perhaps they hoped to find self-esteem through that illusory door. Instead, they smack against a wall of self-degradation and pain, feeling worthless. Instead of experiencing happiness and bliss, they feel sorrow and hurt; and the extramarital relationship may destroy the marriage partner and cause the children pain for a lifetime.

People make mistakes and anyone can suffer from temporary spiritual insanity. But the more people believe in illusions the more insane their thinking becomes. The more they justify their actions and make excuses for the doors they choose or the paths they take, the deeper the insanity becomes and the more they suffer from mental and emotional conflict that destructive tendencies bring.

A HIGHER POWER

There is only one real solution. After people hit the wall enough times, they must recognize that there has to be something or someone outside of themselves that can show them reality, not illusion. Somewhere along the line, they must let go of preconceived notions of what they thought would bring happiness and begin to seek a higher and more powerful entity to lead them on a different path, a power greater than themselves that can bring true sanity, happiness, and spiritual life.

This higher power is available to us all. The power waits diligently for us to call, desiring nothing more than for us to let go of our burdens, stop believing in illusions, and start following a more noble and profound way. This higher power will lead us through the proper door and guide us every step of the way through that crevice and up the mountain. Every step toward the top gives us the sense of self-worth, contentment, happiness, and peace that we've searched for in our lives.

In the beginning, it may be difficult to believe in this higher power. In other twelve-step programs, the higher power is, initially, the group itself. This is a good start. Any higher power is better than the power of our own destructive tendencies. Many people have rejected the notion of God as that power simply because of the teachings in organized religions. They were taught that God is an angry God who will punish them if they do not follow certain teachings or that God is indifferent toward them and their problems. In such cases, it is good that people have left these insidious visions of God behind because they may now be ready to accept the possibility that there is a God of a different nature. We can all learn to believe in a God who loves us no matter what we do, who will never reject us but is always willing to fill us with a wonderful presence. We can come to believe in this power greater than ourselves who created us to have a loving relationship with him and to share that love with our neighbor. That is a God I know I can learn to love, trust, and believe in.

At times, it takes a leap of faith to recognize the reality of God. But it is not a blind leap. It is not the kind of faith where we close our eyes and jump toward God out of fear. A faith based on fear is not a true faith. Rather, this leap of faith is a leap with understanding, not one of blind acceptance or doubt, but one of accepting the possibilities with an open mind.

Swedenborg says there are two types of doubt related to believing or not believing in God: a negative doubt and a positive doubt. Negative doubt leads to spiritual folly and insanity. It believes only what the senses tell us. It says, "I'm going to believe only what I can see, hear, touch, taste, smell, and feel." When we practice this philosophy, we shut the door to spirituality, denying it before we even explore it. We are saying that heaven, hell, God, and whatever we cannot experience with our senses do not exist. With such a philosophy, what is our source of authority? Our lower, more animalistic self with its destructive tendencies tells us what is true according to what feels good. This leads not to a satisfying way of life but to one of frustration and discontent.

Positive doubt, however, does not believe blindly but keeps an open mind. It says, "I don't understand it, but I'm not going to deny it. I will try to live by it to see what happens." The authority here is obvious—a higher authority than ourselves. Moreover, what happens next makes a great difference.

What happens when we have this positive attitude? On a natural level, when we choose to believe in God and his power, we gradually begin to see God in things around us: the beauty of nature or expressions on the faces of others. Then there are the myriads of what seem to be coincidences but are actually planned actions of an invisible but loving force. Phone calls resolving old issues, subtle warnings of dangers, money to pay unexpected bills, voices suggesting alternate courses of action—all these point to a higher power directing the entire worldshow. Most people who have had this kind of experience know what I am suggesting. To experience God's presence does become a bit scary at times. God appears in front of us, as it were, yet leaves us free to see and hear.

That, however, is not the most important part of this process. What is important in our accepting this higher power and allowing him to come into our lives is that we feel his presence within us. It is not something we just imagine. We know! We know God exists because we can feel him. We have felt this awesome power working within us to put down the destructive forces and to set us free from their bondage. The fact that our lives change in dramatic ways is testimony to God's existence. But if we had not believed, these things would never have taken place.

PROOF

Those who are skeptical might ask, "How do I know this will work for me? Am I really going to change if I make this leap in faith and accept a higher power by following these steps?" Returning to the twelve steps for alcoholics and addicts, we can see what these steps have done for other people who suffered greatly from difficulties they could not overcome until they came to believe and trusted in this higher power. If the process works for serious, even devastating problems, why wouldn't it work for those who may be dealing with more subtle shortcomings or day-to-day upsets?

People who came to believe in a power greater than themselves through AA, NA, and other twelve-step groups were not saved from ordinary, petty shortcomings or problems. Some were saved from terrible lives. They weren't saved from simply desiring to take people's possessions; they stole so they could keep their habits going. They weren't saved from a few bouts of sexual fantasy or misconduct. Some were lifted by this power off the streets and into the warmth and safety of a new life. They weren't saved from a lack of self-esteem in their lives; they were saved from utter self-hatred, even from suicide.

Taking the second step really works. Believing in a power greater than themselves has saved many people from the sheer hell they had been experiencing. But we must have enough trust in God to be able to say, "I don't understand them completely, but I'm going to try to live by God's ways." When we do that, our lower self with its destructive inclinations is no longer our authority and guide. The source of power, love, and happiness becomes our authority and our guide. We no longer need to turn off the right path toward fantasy and illusion in our search for happiness. We turn to the truth and that truth makes us free.

When we finally take the right path or walk through the right door, things begin to happen. We realize what sanity really means. Our base feelings no longer rule us and drive us to acts of insanity, anguish, and despair. The higher power within begins to guide us through our own reasoning. We become rational beings capable of making rational choices that lead to goodness, happiness, and peace. That story begins with the next step.

EXERCISES FOR STEP TWO

Separating fact from fiction; recognizing a higher power

1. *Observe your lower self lying:*
    a. *saying to yourself and others what is not true*
    b. *rationalizing, making excuses to yourself*
    c. *exaggerating*
    d. *talking with authority about something you know little or nothing about*

2. *Stop the lying, as soon as you become aware of it.*

3. *Force yourself to talk to God at least once each day and notice the effect this has on your perception of his presence.*

Step Three

Made a decision to turn our will and our lives over to the care of God, as we understood him

BY THE TIME we are ready to take step three, we have come to realize how powerless we are over our destructive tendencies and how insane our actions can be when we follow them. Now it's time to do something with these realizations. We gradually begin to hand over control of our lives to that power greater than ourselves. We begin to "let go and let God."

A PARABLE

An effective illustration for this step is a story from the New Testament. The New Testament is rich with specific symbolism that deals directly with spiritual and psychological development. In fact, Swedenborg says that there is a deeper meaning to all of the Bible that can help us with our spiritual growth. This is especially true of the story of Jesus walking on the water, found in Matthew 14:22–33, because it is a parable about letting go. It contains incredibly important lessons about turning our will and life over to God's care. Think about God as you understand God, but don't reject the story. Although it comes from the New Testament, the story is not just for Christians; symbolically, it illustrates the power of faith. One can learn so much from it.

Immediately after Jesus performed the miracle of feeding five thousand people with five loaves and two fish, he told his disciples to get in the boat and go to the other side of the Sea of Galilee while he prayed on the mountaintop. It was late and darkness was beginning to fall, but the disciples did as Jesus told them, boarding the boat and heading off across the sea to reach the other shore.

Soon, a storm arose. The wind began to roar, and the waves battered the boat so much that the disciples could not reach land. They rowed for a long time, fighting the wind and the waves. They rowed all night in a futile attempt to reach the other side, a mere five miles away. But the wind increased and the waves nearly capsized the boat.

The disciples were afraid; while they struggled to keep the boat afloat, they suddenly saw someone walking on the water toward them. Thinking it was a ghost, they cried out in terror.

But it was Jesus, who calmly called to them, "Be of good cheer. It is I. Do not be afraid." Then Peter, who always seemed to be the spokesman for the disciples, said, "Lord, if it is you, command me to come to you on the water." Jesus said, "Come." Peter stepped out of the boat and began to walk on the water. But his attention drifted as he felt the wind and saw the water whipping around him. He began to doubt. Becoming afraid, he started to sink. "Lord, save me!" he called, and immediately Jesus grabbed him and held him up. He was rescued.

As they boarded the boat, the winds ceased and a calm descended over the sea. Imagine, too, the rays of the morning sun beginning to show forth on the horizon. The disciples in that boat knelt before Jesus in awe.

This is a beautiful and dramatic story. We see Peter's genuine faith and his willingness to let go of the boat and put his trust in Jesus. We also see what happens when faith weakens; even then God helps us. Symbolically, this story touches each of our lives. Jesus, Peter, the boat, the wind, and the waves all symbolize a part of us and our spiritual development.

TAKING THE JOURNEY ALONE

We are all on a journey to serve a purpose, to fulfill a mission, and to find happiness, contentment, and life's meaning. God sends us on this journey, encouraging us to seek these things, promising that he will join us on the other side. Thus, from birth until death, we are on a voyage to find meaning, purpose, and joy.

Each of us has a boat that carries us on life's voyage. Our boat represents our beliefs and our preconceived notions of what life is all about. Our beliefs, chosen from experience, from others, from religion, carry us on the voyage. Each of these beliefs is a section of that boat, and all of them together forms the vessel. In the comfort of these beliefs, we set off on our voyage.

But what often happens? We embark on that journey heedless of who sent us and why we were sent. We leave God or a higher power behind, believing we can reach the goal—find happiness and contentment—without him. As we move into life without him, though, it isn't long before life appears to be working against us. We attempt to change our lives for the better by our own power, but we get nowhere. Destructive tendencies whip up within us like an opposing wind and emotionally blow us in every direction. They prevent us from moving forward toward the goal and the happiness we seek.

The disciples' unsuccessful attempts at rowing all night to reach the other shore symbolize our own powerlessness and destructive tendencies. We may work to change our lives—to be more loving, more peaceful, more content—but without that higher power, we can't do it. Like the disciples, we row and row that boat but get nowhere.

Think about this frustrating sense of impotence. Consider some negative aspects you might want to change in your life, such as a lack of self-esteem. Most of us suffer from personal insecurity at one time or another and know how difficult it is to feel self-assured. We may have read self-help books or used various techniques to gain a sense of self-worth. Maybe we employed affirmations or practiced positive thinking techniques to help us feel better about ourselves. Occasionally, we may have made a little headway until a situation arises—a negative comment from a spouse, a friend, or someone at work—that triggers the sense of insecurity and worthlessness. We are swept back to the place we were before we started working on the problem. We've gotten nowhere.

Perhaps insecurity is not your problem. Instead, you feel a sense of superiority over other people. How do you overcome this air of superiority? Can you say to yourself one day, "Gee, I'm going to stop feeling superior over others today"? If you are really in control, why doesn't this work? You can exert great effort to overcome this dilemma, but where do you start? You can't beat it on your own.

How many people suffer from being perfectionists? Perfectionists can be critical of others and try to show them the "right" way to do a job. But often enough, perfectionists are more dissatisfied with themselves. They can't do a good enough job even when everyone else is satisfied.

Destructive tendencies, therefore, prevent our moving forward toward happiness. We row until we're exhausted from trying to make ourselves happy. Still, we cannot reach the goal on our own.

These tendencies not only hold us back, but they also try to sink us. From time to time they cause great storms in our lives and toss us about unmercifully. We cling to our boat—what we thought was right—tired, frightened, and confused.

For example, twinges of insecurity are inevitable, but insecurity can go beyond a small distraction and turn into self-hatred. We can become angry with ourselves for not being stronger or up to par. Something inside rises up to hurt us. Feelings of self-degradation and even thoughts of self-destruction assault us. We recognize we shouldn't feel this way, but we seem unable to help ourselves because these destructive tendencies whip about in our minds like a storm, assaulting our boat, trying to sink it.

A subtle sense of superiority over other people may not seem to be a problem, but a terrible fear of failure can accompany it. If we believe we are great and put on a front not only before others but also within ourselves, then a quiet inner voice begins to nag: "Well, if you're so great, you'd better not fail." People who suffer from a sense of superiority may also suffer from a terrible fear of failure. They work to do their best in everything they do because they are afraid that, if they don't, their lives might fall apart. If they don't keep rowing their boat, they fear they will sink.

THE PRESENCE WITHIN

During these spiritual storms, we feel alone and in the dark. But we are not alone. That higher power has not abandoned us, but comes to us just as Jesus came to his disciples. Have you ever had that feeling? Perhaps you have gotten into a jam and feel you have failed completely. That is the time when the higher power, the presence within us, appears at a distance. He doesn't push or force himself on us, nor does he call. He simply appears on the horizon of our minds waiting for us to recognize and invite him into our consciousness.

What is this appearance of the presence within? It can be just a sensation that frees us from feeling distraught or alone and abandoned. The presence within may be sensed as a distant promise of inner peace if only we can let go of our turmoil. Often this presence appears in the form of our own conscience, quietly, unobtrusively showing us another way to go in life, so we don't have to rely on our own power to get to the other side.

Remember that the disciples were initially afraid of Jesus when they saw him, yet he represents the presence who had come to help them. And we too may fear that we will have to change if this presence enters our lives. We become afraid that we will lose our own will. Often we want the peace, contentment, and joy that this presence can bring, but we don't want to change our old ways. We want the benefits, but we don't want to make the sacrifice. God's teachings can appear cold and lifeless and a threat that may kill what we believe to be our inner life or deaden our sense of pleasure.

For example, if someone insults us, we are ready to retaliate. But then we hear the words, "Turn the other cheek." These gentle words may frighten us, and we rebel inwardly. "Turn the other cheek? This guy will slap me silly if I turn the other cheek. I can't do that; I'll lose my dignity if I follow that teaching."

Imagine a woman who experienced abusive treatment from her parents as she grew up. She eventually leaves home, but takes with her a great deal of resentment. Then she remembers the phrase, "Forgive and you will be forgiven." That teaching seems frightening as she asks herself, "How can I forgive them? I don't want to be hurt again." These teachings are so frightening that they appear to harm her, not help her. She has trouble seeing their true nature, their inward healing power.

What did Jesus say to his disciples? "Be of good cheer. It is I. Do not be afraid." Goodness emerges from these teachings. We don't turn the other cheek and forgive others just because God indiscriminately chose that way for his own pleasure. It's not a practical joke. Those teachings lead to happiness, to the way to find our God and recognize him.

In the midst of these spiritual storms, we have the opportunity to turn our will and our lives over to the care of God as we understand him, but many of us don't understand him very well. Our concept of God may be very different from what or who God truly is. We have to accept that and be willing to let go of our old ideas.

We may have been brought up believing in a condemning God, a God who is the playground bully who will slap us if we don't play his game. We may be afraid to view God as a loving, caring presence for fear we may be wrong and the condemning God will make us pay for our mistaken ideas. But remember that Jesus spoke to his disciples saying, "Be of good cheer. It is I. Do not be afraid." It is our personal conception of God coming to us, not another's. We have to risk, to change our view of God to a conception more approachable, more realistic about God's true nature.

This revised concept of God may be more difficult for those who have tossed out the idea of a personal God and who view divinity merely as life itself, nature, or perhaps just the power of people. This impersonal view of God tends to picture the power as an "it," a heartless, machine-like quality that negates the building of a genuine relationship. Can you love an "it"? Can you build a relationship with an "it"? You may have to throw out that idea and conclude that God is, indeed, a real force in nature, in spirit, and in human beings, and has an identity and life of his own, with a definite personality.

It is essential to keep the mind open when God presents himself to us. In stormy times, we need to remember that we may be afraid of what we see, but we have to let go of our old concepts of God and see him as he presents himself to us now. When that loving presence comes into our lives in times of turmoil, we may not recognize him as the God we once learned about. Nonetheless, God is still saying, "It is I," that essence of love, that source of goodness, that beautiful being that always meant so much to us. This is the concept of God deep within each of us. It is *your* God coming to *you*.

LETTING GO

When spiritual storms come, we cling to our boat and peer out at this new presence with fear and apprehension, but something inside us recognizes this power and is willing to let go and follow it. We may not always pay attention to this ineffable "something," yet it is there. Within us is a willingness to take the risk, to let go of our preconceived notions, step out of the boat, face the storm, and seek that higher power.

That "something" is our faith, and Peter represents it. He symbolizes our faith, our trust, our hope in that higher power. The faith within us helps us to recall those times when the presence helped us. We remember times of peace when we followed our conscience rather than our destructive tendencies and were willing to let go and let the presence take charge.

Peter said, "Lord, if it is you, command me to come to you on the water." We can envision Peter stepping out of the boat, then walking toward Jesus. This symbolizes our personal letting go, leaving our old ideas behind to seek that presence in our lives. We believe in the power of the presence within and begin to face the storm, to walk to him on the surface of the turbulent sea.

What does walking symbolize in this and other biblical stories? To walk means to live, and this is evidenced throughout the Bible. In Psalm I we read, "Blessed is the man who walks not in the counsel of the ungodly." This doesn't mean we should walk through a board meeting of the National Organization of Atheists. Rather, it means to live a godly life—to follow after God and his ways.

It is important to recognize that getting out of the boat and turning our will over to God does not imply that we turn everything over to God. God doesn't manipulate us like puppets. Peter still had to walk; he was in charge of his actions, but the power of Jesus kept him afloat in the storm. So it is with us. We make the choices, take the actions, and live life to its fullest, but always rely on a new power to sustain and guide us.

Now, for the first time in our lives, we begin to perceive spiritual progress. Emotional waves seem less likely to submerge us, and the violent wind doesn't tear us apart. The presence of this higher power puts us in control of our lives, and we rise above any storm. A miracle seems to take place within us.

We notice this when we meet others who have used the twelve steps to recover from alcoholism or drug addiction. These people tried everything to escape from the storms of their addiction. Not until they let go of their old beliefs and allowed that presence to guide their lives were they able to live a new life without alcohol or drugs. The addiction was gone—perhaps for the first time in ten or twenty years—and along with it the storms. They feel a miracle has taken place; they feel they are walking on water, doing the impossible. This is the first spiritual experience many alcoholics and drug addicts talk about in the twelve-step program—the realization of a miracle in their lives.

All of us can experience this kind of miracle. Suddenly, we are free of the myriad problems we once faced—problems with emotions, with sexual desires, with fears and shortcomings. We seem able to control the problems, led by a power greater than ourselves. We are living a miracle.

We must, however, be realistic. Those feelings of elation at the beginning of a new life don't last forever, and we may lose sight of our goals. We begin to doubt. Peter didn't walk over the water, hug Jesus, and get back into the boat to live happily ever after. Life doesn't work that way. As he walked toward Jesus, Peter began to lose sight of him and began focusing more attention on the whistling of the wind and the whipping of the waves. He was afraid and began to doubt that he could walk on the water. With that doubt he started to sink.

This is symbolic in our own lives. The wind represents the negative thoughts and false ideas that whip around in our minds and howl in our ears during stormy times. Again, we see this throughout the Bible. Jesus says that those who build their house upon the rock will not be hurt by the wind, the rain, or the flood. This is symbolic of those who build their lives on a solid foundation of truth. They will not be hurt by the onslaught of these thoughts during spiritual storms. In contrast, the ungodly are described as chaff that the wind drives away; they experience no higher power and are driven by the wind—their negative thoughts.

In this particular story, the wind that batters Peter denotes negative thoughts. Like Peter, when we initially put our trust in this higher power, we feel we're above the storm. Our initial success and the inner change delight us. But it isn't long before old thought patterns reassert themselves and negativity creeps in. These thoughts insinuate themselves into our minds and make us question our new-found security: "What do you mean you've stopped feeling all that resentment? You've let go of that, huh? Look around; you're being kicked all over the place. People are laughing at you. They're using you. If there's anybody who deserves to feel resentment, it's you." That's the howling wind.

These negative voices whip up emotions, filling us with false ideas that cause fear and doubt. They say, "What is all this about changing your life and being on top of things? You can't change. That's the reality of the situation. Human inadequacy is all there is. There are no such things as miracles. No one can walk on water." It is all too easy to listen to these false ideas and begin to sink back into the way we once were, into selfishness, anger, resentment, depression, guilt, pain, powerlessness, and chaos.

What did Peter do? He was sinking, but he didn't disappear under the murky water or fall in up to his neck and then swim back to the boat a beaten man. (Sometimes we do that, though. It is a genuine relapse into old ways.) Peter remembered who was holding him up; and, like a little child, he looked to Jesus and cried, "Lord, save me." And immediately Jesus took him up.

This represents the ultimate letting go and letting God. There comes the point in our spiritual development when each of us recognizes that we cannot do it ourselves. There comes a point when we realize how powerless we really are over the wind, our negative thoughts; the waves, our emotions; and the storm, our destructive tendencies. We begin to sink into our old way of life and so we cry out to the higher power to save us.

When, in our spiritual turmoil, we call out to the higher power, he is there to help us. He catches us and lifts us into his arms. This presence holds and protects us like a father holding a child, protecting that child from harm. We feel the awesome power of love, a sanctuary from any wind, wave, or storm. This is the ultimate turning of our will and our life over to the care of God as we understand him. This is the ultimate letting go and letting God.

Then Jesus takes Peter and together they get back into the boat. Indeed, we go back to what we believed was right, but this time there is a difference. This time, the presence comes with us and is at the center of our beliefs, at the center of our very being. Moreover, when this happens, a great change occurs. The winds cease and the sea becomes still. The storm is over. Serenity takes its place.

The disciples came and bowed before Jesus, recognizing his power. So too, when we experience God in our lives, everything within us recognizes that not only does this inner presence exist but he is all-powerful, and uses that power for only one purpose: to make us happy by putting our lives in his care.

We can imagine the sun coming up over the horizon; its rays of light glisten on the calm waves and a gentle breeze from a new direction begins to stir and carries with it the message of a new day. It won't be long until we reach the other side.

EXERCISES FOR STEP THREE

Letting go and letting God

1. This week create a task for yourself that relates to handing your life over to the care of God. It might take the form of beginning each day with a prayer such as "God, I give my life to you this day." It could take the form of pausing from time to time to ask: "God, what is your will for me at this moment?" Find a task that applies to the situation of your life at this time.

2. When a stressful situation arises and you feel out of control, ask God to take care of the problem for you: "God, this is now your problem, not mine. But I'll do my best to help you with it."

Step Four

Made a searching and fearless moral inventory of ourselves

THE FIRST THREE STEPS of the twelve-steps program fit together as one unit. They help us recognize the need for a higher power and then help us to begin to turn our lives over to the care of this presence. These beginning steps are critical for spiritual growth because they mark a turning point toward a better way of life. But taking these initial steps is not enough in itself to make deep and lasting changes within us, changes that will bring genuine happiness and spirituality.

TAKING AN INVENTORY

In the first steps, we confessed that we had a need, but did we really understand what that need was? In the beginning of our search for happiness and spirituality, we know that we are unhappy, but we do not know the exact nature of what is causing this unhappy condition. We have only a general idea. In the third step, we turn our will and our lives over to the care of God, but we still don't know exactly what it is that God is going to do for us. We only know in a general way that we need this higher power and that this power can change our lives. Now in step four, we take an inventory of ourselves: we examine ourselves to see exactly what our needs are and how the higher power can help us.

Some people think that a moral inventory is not necessary in order to attain a spiritual life. They think that, if they want spirituality, they simply have to do or believe certain things. Beware of such claims. They aren't realistic. If we merely perform empty acts or believe certain credos without really dealing with our inner motives, we end up avoiding the true problem. To achieve spirituality, we need to fix up our inner selves first and then go forward in life with a new heart to do good things for other people. Isn't that what Jesus meant in Matthew 23:26 when he said, "Cleanse first the inside of the cup and platter"?

What does a company do if its production line produces faulty products? Does it simply increase production to deal with the problem? Of course not; it would only end up with more faulty products. In the same way, if we display some faulty behavior, increasing productivity won't change it. Even going out and doing all sorts of good deeds for people won't take away defective behaviors. Swedenborg says that doing good doesn't cancel out our misbehavior, but rather turns us into hypocrites. We've all heard tales, for instance, of criminal types who spend a lot of money helping the local community or the poor in an effort either to distract the public or to salve their own sense of shame for the wrongs they commit. The fact is, however, that we can't buy our way into heaven when we've made our lives a hell. Doing good doesn't take away evil. But ceasing to do wrong does. If something faulty is coming out of us, we've got to examine it, find out why it has gone wrong, and ask God's help to get rid of the problem. Even as a company would do a complete examination, find the problem on the production line and fix it, we should look inside ourselves first, find the inner fault—the reason that we feel bad about life or that certain things go sour on us—and then work on fixing the problem.

In talking about the spiritual quality of life, Swedenborg makes the following observation in *Divine Providence,* ¶101: "Persons who give no thought to the evils in them, and who do not examine themselves and then desist from the evils, . . . [are] ignorant of what evil is, and . . . love it then from delighting in it." In another work, *True Christian Religion,* ¶564, he states again that "he who has not looked into and searched himself finally ceases to know what damning evil or saving good is." Some might choose to put these ideas in slightly different terms today, but they still express a fundamental truth. Without self-examination, we never really come to see that, indeed, there are destructive forces that motivate us. We may never see the real harm we are causing ourselves and others. We eventually cease to recognize the difference between the positive and the negative, the destructive and the nondestructive, the fundamental difference between good and evil.

We can see this in people who delight in gossiping or telling stories that reflect poorly on others, so that they themselves can feel a sense of superiority. If they never reflect on what they are doing and what the underlying motivation behind their actions is, they cannot see anything wrong with their behavior or any harm that results from it. In fact, they'll go on gossiping day in and day out and justify what they are doing. After a while, they might even begin to think that they are doing a service. They say to themselves, whether consciously or unconsciously, "I'm just letting the truth be known," or "I'm just putting people in their proper light for others to see." They become blinded to their true motivation, which is less than noble. They become blinded to the real harm they are causing others by their actions.

The same need for self-examination applies to all of us. Have you ever been doing something that you considered to be a relatively mundane and harmless thing to do, not interfering with anyone or getting in anyone's way, but then you find out that someone is really upset with what you've been doing or the way you've been doing it? At first you might be taken aback. You wonder what could possibly be the matter with that other person to feel that way. You didn't mean any harm. But then after some personal reflection you realize that, yes, indeed, there were some negative aspects about what you were doing. Lo and behold, there were even some negative motivations behind your actions as well. It's a shocker. It can be very disconcerting to realize that you don't always know how you are affecting others or what is motivating you.

A personal inventory helps us to see these underlying negative motivations that have been causing ourselves and others real harm. It helps us to change for the better in realms we would never recognize without that inventory. For example, picture each of our lives as a beautiful garden with many different flowers, fruits and vegetables, all sorts of good things growing in it. But every once in a while, a weed emerges. The weed may be a form of our selfishness showing through, our greed, our anger, or our impatience that makes our garden look ugly. Sometimes we recognize each of these unwanted weeds, and we just lop off the top of it to get rid of the problem temporarily. Sometimes we just ignore it and hope it will go away. But we don't really deal with the root of the matter.

Sometimes we'll be enjoying the sight of a certain flower in the garden; the next day we notice that it is wilting, and soon it dies. In our symbolic garden, this indicates that something good that we had been doing mysteriously goes bad. Perhaps an important relationship we have had with someone begins to suffer and die. Perhaps it is a good deed gone bad. Something beautiful in our lives just dies or withers away for no apparent reason. Something underneath the surface is killing the good things we love. And this keeps happening until we get in the garden and look beneath the flowers to see what's killing them.

That is what this inventory is all about. It is getting right into the garden, separating the flowers with our hands, and looking underneath to see what is there, to see the weeds that have been choking certain flowers, fruits, and vegetables. With this inventory, we go below the surface to discover the destructive tendencies that have been eating away at our lives, to admit that this garden has other things in it besides vegetables and flowers, to pray to God for the power to begin the work of weeding the garden, and then to get in there and do the job.

It is important that, when we take our moral inventory, we go below the surface. If we want real spirituality, we must look at not only our outer self, our actions, our deeds, but also our inner self, the motives behind those actions. It is not enough for us just to say, "I did this, but I never did that," and work on improving our outward lives alone. We have to look within and see what makes us tick, and what motivates us toward certain actions. If we deal only with the actions but not the feelings behind the actions, we are again just covering over the problem.

A very clear example of this is seen in the alcoholic who has stopped drinking but has gotten no help with the fundamental problems that contributed to his drinking in the first place. Recovering alcoholics who are in a twelve-step program call this sort of individual a "dry drunk." He may have changed his drinking patterns, but he's still the same person on the inside. He still looks for the shortcut or the quick fix. He's still impatient and angry, still guilty and depressed. He seems to exalt in his own sense of self-importance and euphoria. He is still a mess even though he no longer drinks.

Because the alcoholic has never dealt with the real person within, he continues to suffer from the same problems he always had. He may not be drinking anymore, but he is, at heart, still an alcoholic. That is why a twelve-step program is so important for recovering alcoholics. It encourages them to go below the surface and discover the deep-seated problems within. They must learn to think differently than they had in the past. They must learn a new way of living, not only without but within. Only in this way will they truly find a new way of life, a life of true sobriety, a life of peace, serenity, and fulfillment, apart from alcohol.

If we really want to change who we are, then we have to examine our inner self. Not only must our actions be altered but also our loves and motives, which are just as much a part of us as our actions. Sometimes we can love wrong ideas or immoral behaviors but not actually engage in them because we don't want people to think badly of us. Sometimes we may refrain from immoral actions for fear of the law. Stopping ourselves from doing certain destructive actions alone will not change us. We can resist the urge to assault someone but still feel hatred and revenge within. This hatred can be like fire that burns inside. We may refrain from promiscuity but still be plagued with immoral sexual thoughts. We may stop acting on our destructive tendencies but still love those inner urges; and as long as they are not dealt with inside as well as outside, they remain a strong force within and still bring much unhappiness.

HOW TO TAKE AN INVENTORY

There are many ways to take a personal moral inventory. Helpful guides are available from different twelve-step groups. The method for taking the fourth step is your own choice, but there are guidelines. A moral inventory takes time. Reserve several hours for the initial inventory to settle your thoughts and to do some quiet reflection. This won't be completed in one day. Most guides suggest that, after completing an inventory, you put the list away for a while and return to it later; you may want to make additions.

The inventory should be a written one since there is a great difference between superficially counting off one's shortcomings or deeds and writing them down for later reflection. Writing them gives a more objective view.

What should you write about yourself? There are many different approaches, but you might want to start with a brief life history. Some people begin with childhood, writing about their reactions to events in their life. They might write, "Senior year in high school: suspended for dismantling teacher's car; Feelings: arrogance, embarrassment, resentment." Perhaps you will list five or six other significant events that occurred during that year.

The next heading could be, "College: First year," followed by a list of noteworthy deeds and the accompanying feelings. This inventory could embrace all of the college years, first job, marriage, a year-by-year recounting of your life.

Some people write two lists: their positive character traits and their negative ones. Others use the familiar "seven deadly sins"—pride, greed, lust, anger, gluttony, envy, and laziness—as a base from which to work. Whether or not you believe in the traditional concept of sin, these are some of the more universal destructive tendencies or character defects. Still others picture their feelings as different products on the shelf at the grocery. They decide which "products" are getting too much space, which shouldn't be on the shelf at all, are neglected, underpriced, or sold out. The idea should be clear. Any of these techniques can serve the purpose when you do a moral inventory.

How do you discover your inner motives? There are several ways. Besides remembering and recording what you have done, begin paying attention to your trend of thought when you are alone. Are your thoughts unselfish and constructive or selfish and destructive? Be honest and ask yourself, "What would I do if there were no laws nor anyone to judge me?"

Perhaps life would be no different for you under these circumstances. On the other hand, maybe you sense that some destructive tendencies would readily seek expression if there were no outward restraints. If you could rob a bank and know for certain you wouldn't be caught, would you do it? Ask yourself, "What do I see as allowable? Does it match up with what other people believe is allowable? Does it match up with the teachings of most religions? If not, why not? Am I fooling myself?" When you ask these questions, you begin to see beyond the superficial self into deeper motivations, the bad ones and the good ones.

Don't look at just the negatives when you take your moral inventory; that approach will only depress you and make you want to give up. Get a balanced picture of yourself; recognize the positive as well as the negative. The only reason you are looking for these destructive tendencies is to deal with them and make your life better, not to berate yourself.

Even though, for practical reasons, the focus is usually more on the negative than on the positive, don't lose sight of the positive. A gardener who is weeding a garden will not forget that there are other things in the garden besides rampant weeds. The short-term focus may be on the weeds; but after they have been rooted out, the garden thrives, displaying beautiful flowers and lush fruit and vegetables. That is the desired outcome.

When I attended the Academy of the New Church, a religious high school outside Philadelphia, a minister there brought this concept home to me. He was my religion teacher and a recovering alcoholic who knew how to talk to the students on their level. I remember distinctly his bringing home this point about getting a balanced picture of yourself. He said, "When you do this self-examination, look for the good points and the bad points to get a balance. Write these things down." I remember trying to trick the man—which high school kids are wont to do—by asking, "Sir, what if you don't have any good in you? What should you do then?"

He smiled and in a harsh, somewhat sarcastic voice said, "Schnarr, did you ever kick your grandmother down the stairs?"

"No," I replied.

"Then write that down!" he exclaimed.

There is a point to that simple, somewhat sarcastic answer. Sometimes we get into mindsets where we see just the bad; we find it difficult to acknowledge the good we do. If you have to, write down the things you haven't done; those too are important. It doesn't hurt to remind ourselves of our own good, especially when we're feeling depressed or guilt-ridden over our condition. I might say to myself, "Yes, I have a problem with my temper, but I've never hurt anyone. I argue a lot, but I try to be fair and am generally a forgiving person. I don't hold grudges." We might list our good qualities next to the shortcomings, then say to ourselves, "Yes, I am hardheaded; I argue; I look for the quick fix in life; I am an egotist; I have a short temper. But I am also optimistic, fair, basically honest, and industrious." This provides a balanced picture and helps us to maintain a sense of hope as we recognize the shortcomings that exist in our lives.

As step four states, this inventory is intended to be not only searching but also fearless. Why fearless? Because we have turned our will and our lives over to the care of God before taking this step. This moral inventory is not the first step because we need that higher power when we take it; that makes it a fearless inventory.

We have already called on the higher power to help us. We have called on God to give us the strength to overcome destructive tendencies. Now we are in his care when we begin to take a hard look at ourselves. He will supply us with courage and hope as we take this inventory and discover the destructive tendencies within. The knowledge may be frightening, and we will discover things about ourselves that won't be attractive or noble. But the presence within will comfort and encourage us. He tells us destructive tendencies do not have to motivate us. He tells us that we can change—with his help. We will receive new inclinations and loves for good and useful purposes. Along with these, order, peace, and joy will come into our lives. It is important to have that higher power with us when we make this change.

One minister I know has an illustration he uses in teaching children and young people. He draws a picture of a tiny person next to a huge monster. He tells the children, "If you're all alone and are looking at those frightening things within you, you feel like a midget looking up at this looming monster." Then he adds an even larger figure of God behind the tiny person, saying, "But when you recognize that God is with you, you may still feel very small, but you're holding the hand of a big and powerful person who far overshadows this monster. You immediately realize this monster does not have any power over you at all." When our higher power accompanies us during this inventory, we can face anything. We realize that, in his presence, the power of destructive tendencies shrinks.

After writing a list of the bad and the good within us, we need to take time to review the list to be sure we have covered the entire gamut of our inward lives. We ask ourselves whether we've been honest in our appraisal. We must be ruthless in the search to discover ourselves and hold nothing back. If some problem areas are left untouched or undocumented, those problems will not just go away. Brutal honesty spares us much pain down the road by dealing with the inner problems now. Keep in mind that the higher power is with us to protect us from harm and to comfort us during this stressful time of soul-searching.

After the fourth step, not only are we relieved but we also experience another new sensation sweeping over us: a feeling of awe as we sense a new reality. Those grand illusions of ourselves vanish with this step. Egotists feel what life is like without a suffocating ego. They can breathe for a change; it feels good to be humble. Those who suffer from overwhelming guilt realize they are not so bad after all. They are wrapped in a sense of peace as they come to accept themselves. It is an awe-inspiring moment to feel neither pride nor guilt, to have no grand illusions, to know the truth about self—and this for the first time.

EXERCISE FOR STEP FOUR

....

Preparing for a fearless inventory

Find one-half hour this week to sit quietly and list five emotions, behaviors, or recurring thoughts that you know are liabilities to your spiritual growth. Then list another five emotions, behaviors, or recurring thoughts that you consider assets to your spiritual growth. In doing this project, notice any new insights or discoveries.

Step Five

Admitted to God, to ourselves, and to another human being the exact nature of our wrongs

STEPS FOUR AND FIVE go hand in hand. After discovering the nature of our wrongs, it is critical to admit them to God, self, and another person. It is critical for two reasons, which may seem contradictory.

First, we confess these shortcomings so that we can accept responsibility for them. Second, by accepting responsibility for them, we can let them go and begin to break free of their grip and the burdens they have placed on us.

Without this step, it would be easy to take a cursory look at our shortcomings and then move on with life, never really accepting these flaws as our own, never really dealing with them in a constructive way. Perhaps you've had someone point out one of your shortcomings. Have you listened to the criticism, taken note of it, even thought about it for a while, then found that, as time passed, the criticism slipped away and you continued on as before? That has been my experience.

My wife, Cathy, told me that I spend too much time at work and tend to put family matters in the last place of importance. I heard that criticism, thought about it, even acknowledged its validity; but, as days passed, I got caught up in ministry again, completely forgetting Cathy's complaint. I continued to behave in my customary way until she'd bring the problem to my attention once again. Nothing changed until I finally got serious and took time to reflect not only on my behavior but also to admit my fault: "Yes, I tend to put work before family." This admission made a big difference. I realized I had heard the problem and, unconsciously perhaps, toyed with the idea, but I didn't take responsibility for it. Admitting my neglect to myself made it easier to actually do something about it because it became real. Admitting my failing to God helped me see the reality of the situation and gave me strength to deal with it.

Admitting the problem to Cathy also made it easier for me to begin to deal with it. Stating it to another person and promising to deal with it has more power than merely acknowledging it to oneself. I found myself compelled to take action because I had openly taken the responsibility and had promised to try to change my priorities. It has made a difference. This shortcoming, as well as many others, still surfaces from time to time; but since I recognize its existence, I am better able to handle it realistically and thus make progress.

There are good reasons that we should admit the nature of our wrongs not only to ourselves but also to another person and to God. You ask, "Why must we admit our shortcomings to God? Doesn't he already know them?" This is a valid question. God does know us—better than we know ourselves. He knows all of our shortcomings well, but if we don't acknowledge these shortcomings personally and take responsibility for them, he can't help us. He will not interfere with our freedom or take anything away from us that we do not acknowledge and consciously desire to remove.

We see this principle in many biblical stories. Why did God ask Adam and Eve what they had done after they ate the forbidden fruit? Didn't he already know? Of course he did, but God asked them so they would reflect on their actions and take the responsibility. Many times Jesus questioned those who were noticeably ill, "What do you want me to do for you?" or "Do you wish to be made well?" It makes little sense that Jesus asked these questions until we recognize that each of these people, on a spiritual level, represents us. The sick had to acknowledge their need, obvious though it may have been.

A basic principle is expressed here that applies to each of us. The blind, the sick, and the lame symbolize ourselves in times of inner blindness, sickness, and infirmity. Jesus' healing of these people symbolizes the spiritual healings God performs on us. But before he can heal our spiritual infirmities, we have to recognize them, admit that we have a problem, and ask for help. That is how to open the way for his healing power. By confessing our shortcomings to God, we are in effect saying, "God, I am blind; help me to see. I am sick; make me well. I am unable to live in your ways; help me that I might walk." Confession—inviting God in to heal us—brings about union with God.

Swedenborg offers another, more spiritual reason to make confession before God. He says that such a confession brings about a oneness with God and allows God to make the necessary changes within us. As he writes in his short work *Charity*, ¶206, "The confession of one's sins before the Lord brings about conjunction with Him, and a reception of influx from Him. . . . The Lord then operates through the person's inmost things right down to the outmost, and removes the lusts that are the roots of evil."* When we confess those inner destructive cravings before him, God is then able to come into our being in a new way and to get at the root of our dysfunctions. God becomes the gardener within our spiritual garden, removing what is harmful and nurturing what is good and useful to growth.

Admitting the nature of our wrongs to God and to ourselves gets us started on the path to spiritual growth. But we might wish to confess these things to another person. Why? Because it is an opportunity to bring our total personality into full light, giving us the most objective view of ourselves that we have ever encountered. Confessing to another human being forces us to take a hard look at our problems and gives a truly balanced picture of ourselves.

Often, after doing some difficult soul-searching, we find ourselves becoming introverted, prone to isolating ourselves from others. Perhaps our

---

*Emanuel Swedenborg, *Charity*, tr. F. F. Coulson (London: Swedenborg Society, 1947). This work has also been published as *Charity: The Practice of Neighborliness*, tr. W. F. Wunsch, 2nd edition (West Chester, Pennsylvania: The Swedenborg Foundation, 1995); however, ¶206 is not contained in this version, as is explained in the "Introduction" to that volume, p. xvii.

problems make us feel we are worse than others. We may think our problems are unique; no one else can understand them. We tend to deny some shortcomings and place too much stress on others. For example, we might consider a lack of initiative our biggest problem when, actually, it is an indifference toward others. Or introspection may suggest that a fear is our obstacle instead of a selfishness that holds us back.

When we risk opening our hidden selves to another, we are forced to acknowledge the effect our spiritual life has on others. No longer alienated from the human race, we relate our inner lives to all humanity.

Beyond this, we see another human being respond to our problems with a different point of view; thus, we become less myopic. There is comfort in knowing others who share similar shortcomings and can understand us, show compassion, and offer help.

A woman pointed this out to me. She always felt motherhood brought out her greatest failings. She believed she was a terrible mother to her three children because she yelled at them, didn't give them enough individual attention, neglected to teach them, and couldn't give them enough love. She knew other women who appeared to be "supermoms," doing everything right, creating a wonderful life for their children. Why couldn't she be more like them? The maternal instinct, or her lack of it, topped her list of shortcomings.

When she reached step five in her recovery program and admitted her shortcomings to God, herself, and especially to another person, her perspective about her parenting changed. She went to a counselor who, having raised a family of her own, related a few of her own experiences and blunders as a mother. They laughed together, and the woman finally began to feel that she really wasn't such a bad parent after all; the counselor herself wasn't a perfect mother. Finally, the counselor shared an article on the foibles of parenting and recommended a support group for parents. After taking that fifth step, the woman felt better about herself. With a new resolve, she began to tackle some of her parenting problems.

The support that comes from another is a boon not only to our spiritual life in general but to our self-perception in particular. What we now think is a major problem may be minimized after discussion with a trusted person. On the other hand, what now appears to be insignificant may, in reality, need immediate attention. Talking about specific problems can be therapeutic and enlightening. Often, in this fifth step, the person who listens to us asks questions that clarify troublesome issues, helps us face ourselves honestly, and encourages us to make needed changes to achieve a better life.

If you are apprehensive about taking step five, perhaps my story will alleviate some of your fears and help you recognize the real benefits of this process.

I had taken a good personal inventory—about eighteen pages of notes. By the way, this is typical of one of my shortcomings; I tend to overdo everything. If the step instructed me to be exact in my calculations then, by golly, I was going to be exact, and then some! I was eager to complete step five, admitting shortcomings to God and to myself. But to talk to another person about my problems wasn't so easy. At that time, someone suggested that I seek out a professional—a minister, priest, psychologist, or counselor—who was familiar with the twelve-step program.

I chose a highly recommended Catholic priest who had heard many fifth-step confessions. Already apprehensive, I found that his name offered little comfort: it was Father Scary. His name was appropriate for how I was feeling, but it didn't fit his character. He was open, warm, and attentive.

As I began to express my shortcomings with a brief explanation of the more glaring ones, I felt naked, helpless, and vulnerable. It was not a comfortable feeling. I pictured Father Scary laughing uncontrollably, pointing at me, and saying, "You're a minister? Ha! Ha! Ha! . . . Your church is pretty desperate, huh? If you're the minister, I'd hate to meet the members of your congregation! Boy, my friends are never going to believe this one when I tell them. . . ."

Of course, that didn't happen. Instead, my confessor listened intently, and laughed and frowned *with* me but not *at* me. Father Scary added such phrases as "Gee, I remember when I did that," or "Gosh, you're making me feel bad. I still have a problem with that one." He also gave me advice here and there to help me overcome some of the challenges. By the time I had my say I felt at ease; in fact, I felt wonderful. Not until I completed the fifth step did I really understand what it was all about.

I walked out of the church with a new view of myself and a new resolve. I wasn't the worst person who ever lived nor was I the greatest. Neither was I special in any way: I had no major problems that others don't encounter from time to time. I had no powers or insights or abilities that exceeded the ordinary person. I discovered that I was "normal"—much like everyone else who makes mistakes from time to time, needs God's help, and has the potential to be a good person. But more than this, through the fifth step, I accepted responsibility for the flaws in my character and, in so doing, received the strength to deal with them. I left Father Scary with a new lease on life. No longer burdened with the baggage of guilt, fears, inhibitions, bad memories, and pain, I was invigorated with a new enthusiasm to carry me through the remaining steps.

That is the beauty of the fifth step. By accepting the responsibility for our shortcomings by confessing before God, ourselves, and another human being, we let go of old hang-ups and become willing to start again. We see the potential for destruction in our lives, but we also see the potential for vast goodness, usefulness, fulfillment, and joy.

In taking the fifth step, we lay ourselves on the line. Confessing our shortcomings to another human being offers perspective and objectivity. Confessing them to ourselves helps us accept responsibility for them. Confessing them to God readies us to receive his help in removing them from our lives. We leave step five with new vision, but we will return to it from time to time as we change, grow, and discover even deeper parts of ourselves. Once we were blind; now we see. Once we felt crippled and lame, now we find new strength and vitality to follow our God. With this new strength of purpose and vision, we move forward with confidence and resolve to begin a new life.

EXERCISES FOR STEP FIVE

....

Learning to open oneself to God, to self, to others

1. Think about one destructive tendency within yourself that has occasionally harmed others. Go to a private place (e.g., your bedroom, bathroom, car) and say to God, "I admit I have a tendency to _____ ; it is a destructive tendency. Help me to recognize it."

2. Choose either the same or another destructive tendency, admit it to God, then find a mirror. Look into the mirror and say to yourself, "I confess that I have a tendency to and that it is hurtful to others. I have confessed this to God and to myself and am ready to begin to face this problem."

3. Find someone you trust and share with them a minor transgression you have committed lately. Notice how you feel.

(Tasks 1, 2, and 3 are a sampling of how to work step five. If you're really serious about spiritual growth, take your inventory to a professional and start serious counseling.)

Step Six

Became entirely ready to have God remove all these defects of character

WE HAVE COME a long way. Working through the first five steps, we have made many discoveries about ourselves. We have seen good things and have recognized flaws. We are aware of the vast potential for spiritual growth, but at the same time recognize destructive tendencies that could lead to disaster. We have acknowledged these tendencies and the consequent actions that bring pain to ourselves and others. We have admitted our flaws before God and another human being. In step six, we prepare to remove these defects of character and begin a new life.

A POSITIVE PROCESS

Focusing on our character defects, admitting them, and then asking God to remove them from us may appear to be a negative process. But these steps are really not negative. Quite the contrary, they are truly positive, as anyone who has practiced them will testify. We return to the analogy of the garden with beautiful flowers as well as choking weeds. Is weeding that garden a positive or a negative process? It may be a difficult and tedious task with a short-term focus on the bad, but the end result is a positive one. A gardener removes the weeds and the garden flourishes.

And what about the company that finds a defect on the production line? Is it a negative action to locate the defect and then fix it? There is, of course, a time of analysis with a focus on a specific problem, but this is only temporary until the problem is resolved and the company resumes production.

What if we are suffering from cancer? Is it a negative process to diagnose it, isolate it, and then remove it? Obviously, it is a positive procedure. So it is with our spiritual growth. It may be difficult—even painful—to recognize defects, admit them, and remove them from our lives; but the end result is a beautiful, blossoming life. We become good, useful, and spiritually healthy human beings. Nothing is more positive than that.

A priority in spiritual growth should be to rid oneself of shortcomings. This takes precedence over prayer, meditation, good deeds, reconciliation, everything! Why? Because for every character defect we remove, its opposite—virtue—takes its place. Think about that. Take away hate and love replaces it. Take away greed and benevolence takes its place. Take away pride and humility takes its place. Take away disorder and order takes its place. Becoming ready to have God remove these defects of character and actually having them removed are the crux of this twelve-step program. When we remove hate, pride, greed, and disorder, God takes their place for God is goodness, love, benevolence, and order. This is how God enters into us and affects us.

Sometimes we think of God as a self-contained entity with no relationship to us except that he created us, deposited us in the world, and tells us how to live. We often experience God as an obscure, elusive being. But God really is love, and when love enters our hearts, we allow God to enter. God is peace, joy, and serenity. Every good we experience mirrors God within us. We are not God, but God can dwell with us and within us. Revelation 3:20 bears this out: "Behold I stand at the door and knock. If any man hear my voice and open the door, I will come into him and sup with him and he with me." How essential it is, then, to remove those things that are contrary to God so God can replace them.

Swedenborg describes the process of removing our shortcomings as taking away the barriers that impede the inflow of the Divine within us. The light shines because the darkness has been removed. When we become entirely ready to have God remove our defects of character—and then *allow* God to do so—the Divine flows in and opens us up to spiritual influence from heaven. Our conscious minds become ordered, illuminated, cleansed of defects, and raised up into a new spiritual state. Swedenborg says this in his short work *The Doctrine of Life*, ¶86 [4]:

> So long as a person does not shun evils as sins, the [lusts] of evils block up the interiors of the . . . mind, on the part of the will, . . . like a thick veil there, and like a black cloud beneath the spiritual mind, and they prevent its being opened. But . . . the very moment a person shuns evils as sins, the Lord inflows from heaven, takes away the veil, dispels the clouds, opens the spiritual mind, and so introduces the person into heaven.*

We can see how important this step is: it opens us up to heaven.

BECOMING ENTIRELY READY

Steps six and seven—becoming ready to remove these defects and then asking God to remove them—are closely related. One might even wonder why a step for getting ready is necessary. Can't we move directly to get rid of these character defects? No, because getting ready to change requires time; we must prepare for the changes to come. We want to be entirely ready for God to remove defects of character, but that is not easy.

After all, we are quite attached to many of these character defects. Of course, we are ready to shed those that cause us immediate pain, but we are less inclined to let go of those we are comfortable with. They are a part of us that gives delight. The delight may be a quick fix or a cheap thrill that ultimately leads to unhappiness, but we suffer from this insanity occasionally. We cling to things that are often bad for us. Asking God to remove some unwanted shortcomings may be easy, but we may cling to others more tenaciously.

---

*Emanuel Swedenborg, *Doctrine of Life*, in *Four Doctrines*, tr. J.F. Potts, 2nd ed. (West Chester, Pennsylvania: Swedenborg Foundation, 1997).

For instance, we recognize in ourselves the tendency to "lord it over" people at work. We act like the big shot, insisting that our way is the only way, never admitting mistakes, never giving others a break. We might want God to remove this defect since we sense that co-workers don't appreciate or like us very much. We've struggled with our own impertinence and know what a fool we can make of ourselves. We can say quite readily, "God, take this from me; I don't want to be like this anymore!" On the other hand, we may be less ready to deal with other shortcomings on the workfront. We may have found an easy way to pad our expense account and make a few extra dollars on the side. Having grown accustomed to spending this illicit money, it's hard to give up this practice. We willingly give up the one shortcoming, but grudgingly forsake the other.

Perhaps we suffer from guilt, fear, or depression, and would gladly rid ourselves of these feelings. But we cling tenaciously to self-pity, self-centeredness, or contempt for others. To relinquish greed, hunger for power, or vindictiveness may be easier than letting go of sexual fantasies, manipulative practices, or a sense of self-importance. If we are truly serious about our spiritual growth, we must let go of all of our defects.

Sometimes we believe we're ready to give up certain shortcomings or at least their consequences, but we never attempt to deal with the actual problem. We work hard at changing the effects of the shortcomings but avoid the root of the problem.

For instance, consider a man who has an alcohol problem. He comes home drunk night after night. He can't carry on a normal conversation at the dinner table. He has only derogatory comments for his son. He asks, on cue every night, "Have you done your homework? Isn't it time for you to go to bed? What the hell are you doing watching TV if your homework isn't done!" Once in awhile, when he has really tied one on, he pulls out his belt and raps his son across the back of the legs to speed him into his bedroom. Other times, he's too hung over to attend his son's ball games or to work with the son on a school project. By the time he feels good enough to get going again, he hits the bottle, then goes to the games loaded, loud, and belligerent, making a fool of himself and embarrassing his child. Or he tries to help his son with a project and ends up ruining the whole thing.

In the morning, when this man awakes, he knows what hell he is causing his family. The guilt and depression are almost enough to kill him. He cries that his son does not have the father he could have. He wishes he could change. So he decides that he will change. He will show his son that he is a good dad and that he does care. Thus he begins a new life. Instead of coming home drunk and belligerent, he comes home drunk and with a gift in his hand. He slaps his son on the back and says in a loud, slurred voice, "Here son, I brought you a present. It's a new baseball glove." After dinner he insists that they have a catch but can hardly stand up to go out the back door. Night after night he either brings his son a gift or drags him to a baseball game or bowling, or to a movie. He even lets his son stay up as late as he wants, with just a few subtle derogatory comments, and raises the boy's allowance.

Perhaps the son would never dare come out and say what he is thinking. If he could find the courage to talk to his dad, he would tell him how he felt and what he really wanted. He might say, "Please, please, listen to me. I don't want to be able to stay up all night. I don't want your money. I don't want any more baseball mitts or other stupid gifts. I don't like bowling. I'm tired of baseball games. I don't want to see any more movies. I just want my dad. I just want my dad!"

Alcoholics are good examples of people who work on the periphery of their lives trying to change but never tackling the root of the problem. But we all do this to one degree or another. We see a problem. We may even decide we are going to change. But since we never became entirely ready to deal with it, we work very superficially on its effects and the cause goes untouched.

If we want spiritual growth, we can't attack a problem halfheartedly. We must become entirely ready to have God remove not just one or two but *all* of our defects. There will be some we do not readily wish to have removed, but they must go too. There will be other defects that may not seem to cause immediate harm, but deep inside we know that they do. At one time or another we have recognized the insanity of following those destructive inclinations. We know the delight is short-lived. We have felt the deep pain after the thrill is gone. We have seen the suffering they bring. They all have to be removed.

The primary reason we must become entirely ready to have God remove all of our shortcomings is that we won't really grow spiritually if we consciously decide to hold onto certain ones because we like them. We turn our spiritual growth into a sham. The character defects we choose not to deal with will simply take the place of the others. They may even rekindle the flaws we thought we had dealt with and removed. We have to make the decision to have them removed in full or the changes are in vain.

To illustrate the reason that we need to let go of these destructive tendencies absolutely, let's personify them and call them "Mr. Hyde." We may like to be thought of as Dr. Jekyll, but there is a Mr. Hyde in all of us. Mr. Hyde is the epitome of everything undesirable within us. He is responsible for every character defect or destructive inclination we suffer from. If left to rule within us, Mr. Hyde would lie, steal, kill to get his way. We'd like to get rid of Mr. Hyde because he causes havoc in our lives whenever he comes out.

How do we get rid of him? The twelve steps give a simple answer. Recognize him, take responsibility for letting him act out in your life, become entirely ready to have him removed, and pray to God to remove him. Sounds simple? It is, and the wonderful thing is, it works! The problem though, is that if we don't become entirely ready to have him removed, he isn't going to go. You can't ask for part of him to go and yet hold onto the other part of him. You can't say, "I'd like him to stop hating, but he can keep stealing." You can't say, "I don't want him to fill me with fears, but if he wants to use people, that's fine." If we hold onto part of our destructive tendencies, we don't completely release the rest of them. It's like kicking Mr. Hyde out but holding onto his coattails at the same time.

If we renege on our pact with God and deal with only part of our problems, we do not change for the better. If we stop lording it over people but refuse to deal with our sense of pride, we get nowhere. After a matter of time, our pride leads us back to acting out our old behavior patterns. What if we deal with our deceitfulness because we find that easy but won't let go of greed? Are we really changing for the better or are we fooling ourselves? Isn't the greed going to lead us back to deceitfulness? If we ask God to remove something like our fears but refuse to let him touch our contempt for others, are we really dealing with the total destructive self within us? Are we growing spiritually?

Now this doesn't mean that if we work on only one fault, we aren't going to make progress. We can weaken Mr. Hyde's power by dealing with even one of our shortcomings. It doesn't mean that if we don't recognize a particular shortcoming within us, we won't be able to deal with and eventually remove those we do see. We will make progress. What it means is if we are *serious* about spiritual growth, we must be willing to go all the way. Do we want Mr. Hyde to go or to stay? Do we want God to change us or don't we? We can't have it both ways.

Let one more illustration suffice. If a person is suffering from cancer and God is the surgeon, the person can't say, "OK, God, remove this part of the cancer and that part, but don't touch the cancer over there." Perhaps God can come in and do the work where the person will let him, but sooner or later the untreated cancer will infiltrate and eventually kill the body. If we are serious about spiritual growth, then let's tell the doctor, "Do what you gotta do," and let him take care of it.

Once we reach the decision to change, we turn ourselves over to God to do whatever he must to change us. We open the way for changes to take place within us, and deal with one character defect at a time. Some will re-emerge from time to time, but with a full commitment, we allow God to make changes wherever necessary.

How do we become entirely ready to have God remove our character defects? We simply do our best. We don't claim spiritual perfection, but we claim spiritual progress. And that is an important point to remember. We can strive for perfection, but achieving it is an ideal. Only God is the perfect being. All we can do is try. We can be honest with ourselves, look at all facets of our life, and ready ourselves for God to work in us. If we are willing to cooperate with God in beginning a new life, then we are ready for step seven.

We may be afraid that, if we let go of all of these character defects, we may no longer feel like ourselves. We may fear that, if we let God in to make so many changes, we will lose our sense of self. You will see for yourself that your fears are unfounded when you commit yourself to these steps. Swedenborg says that to the degree that we recognize that all things are from God and allow him to come into us and fill us with his presence, we do not lose our sense of self but, on the contrary, we gain more of a sense of self. The more we let God in to make the necessary changes the more we will feel like ourselves. Not only will we feel like ourselves more than ever before, but we will experience more happiness, contentment, and self-worth than we have ever dreamed about.

I once met a woman at a twelve-step meeting who summed it up: "I don't know much but I do know one thing. There is a God and it ain't me." That, my friend, is the beginning of wisdom. There will be times when we are afraid to let go of some of those things within us that seem to be so much a part of ourselves. But we don't need to be afraid. Trust in that higher power. Give God a chance. Let him do what is necessary for you to grow. In reality, you have nothing to lose, and everything to gain.

EXERCISES FOR STEP SIX

Loosening up to let God change you

1. Think of one character defect or shortcoming that you really don't want to let go. Analyze the reasons for your hesitancy. Determine how this particular defect hurts you.

2. On a specific day, blot out one pet shortcoming. Examples: Try not to tell one lie; abstain from criticizing others. Was it easy? How can you make yourself ready to let God make those changes for you?

Step Seven

Humbly asked God to remove our shortcomings and began a new life

HUMILITY IS ESSENTIAL for spiritual growth. We don't stand a chance at achieving any constructive spiritual change or growth without it. If we are full of our own self-importance, God cannot enter in because there is no room for him. When we become proud and egotistical, we fully believe we are the source of all our happiness, the master of our fate, the creator and redeemer of our own lives. With such an attitude, it doesn't take long for our spiritual lives—even our earthly lives, for that matter—to come crashing down on us.

I once heard a remarkable man talk at an open AA meeting about humility and his hard-earned knowledge of it. He was a stockbroker and a recovering alcoholic. He admitted that, before he found AA and the twelve-step program, he was probably the most egotistical person anywhere. He had entered the world of stocks and bonds at a time that the market was taking off, and he had made a fortune picking stocks for his clients.

During his drinking "career," he spent most of his time picking and choosing stocks on a drunken whim more than on any fact sheet or analysis. Like so many "charmed drunks," he was extremely lucky and didn't lose money. Every stock he picked went up; as they went up, his own sense of importance went up. At that time he believed himself to be the most successful broker in the country and that he would die a rich, famous man. Moreover, people treated him like a great oracle of old—

associates, friends, even his boss came to him for counsel. He was given responsibility for the largest accounts in the company, and this whiz-kid of Wall Street doubled and tripled its money.

As he escalated to the top, he bought a mansion with a pool, two new cars, and all the toys less-affluent people only dream about. Every Saturday night his mansion turned into a party palace where he hosted a grand victory celebration.

During one of these parties, after he had six or seven cocktails, the president of a foreign oil company phoned him, quite upset upon hearing news about a certain stock that this broker had bought for the company. It seems the news could make a large difference in this oil company's assets, making or breaking the company. The broker was so drunk that he could understand only a few sentences the executive, with his foreign accent, was speaking. He did hear the man say repeatedly, "Should we buy more or sell? Should we buy or should we sell?" The broker, wanting to get back to the party, simply put the phone to his chest, hesitated, then came back to the phone and said, "Sell." He hung up and went back to the party.

When the stockbroker told this story, he admitted that he could just as easily have said "Buy." He had kept hearing "buy or sell," "buy or sell." "I guess the last word I heard was 'sell' so I said 'sell.'" The next day the stock plummeted. His client could have lost a fortune; the man called him later, almost in tears. He praised the broker and kept saying, "Thank God. Thank God." Finally, the broker, in a wave of egomania said, "God? Thank God? Don't thank God! Thank me!" This was the peak of his arrogance. "Don't thank God! Thank me!" He thought he was God.

What happened next is typical when people begin to think they really are God and that nothing can shatter their reign of glory. The broker made a bad selection in stocks—and then another and another and still another. Then the market crashed in October 1987, and he hit bottom in a matter of weeks. At the same time, he came to the realization that he was not only an alcoholic who desperately needed help, but he was nothing at all without God. Only God could bring him back to sanity and a balanced picture of himself and his life.

Today he is an average broker, but one who is happy for the first time and is making it in life. He admits he has something far more valuable than monetary wealth. He has humility.

I don't particularly feel sorry for this man and the mistakes he made, but his story illustrates what pride and conceit can do. They blind a person to the truth about self and life. They cause a person to make incredible mistakes. They put the person's ego in the place of God, blocking him so completely out of life that he cannot possibly help or change the person. Perhaps the only thing that helped this man spiritually was to lose the whole world to gain his own soul.

If we have sincerely taken step one of this program, our inward lives will have little in common with that stockbroker and his ordeal. But during the course of working these steps, we need to keep a humble heart. If we don't, we will overlook some of our more critical character defects. When we begin the process of asking God to change us, we won't let him make the changes. We'll try to make the changes ourselves without his help, and the result will be failure. We need God; we need to recognize that we need God. Without that recognition, we're back to square one.

If we have worked the first six steps of this program faithfully, we will be humbled. We will know our powerlessness over the destructive tendencies within us. We will see how our sanity is challenged without a higher power to guide us. Having let go of old ideas, we will have begun to listen to a higher voice. Through a personal inventory and confession, we have identified our character defects and have taken measures to work on removing those defects. We know humility.

Humility is used in this step to remind us that we will still be tempted to tackle our character defects alone—without God's help. However, as we have seen in step one, we don't have the power to handle these destructive tendencies. We can fight against them, but we can't overcome them—not until we allow God to fight the battle for us.

COOPERATING WITH GOD

Asking God to remove our shortcomings isn't enough. We have to do our part and cooperate with him to allow these changes to take place. The all-powerful God makes the changes, but we allow him to make them through our actions. At times it may seem that we are acting by ourselves, yet we fully recognize that God is making the changes within us.

To strengthen this concept, call to mind an alcoholic who, drink in hand and between gulps, asks God to stop him. Or consider how many people with uncontrollable appetites have stuffed their faces with the third slice of pizza, paused for a moment, and asked God to stop them from eating so much. People who suffer from these compulsions will admit that it happens, but God can't help them until they begin to help themselves. Alcoholics have to awaken in the morning and walk past that bottle to get some help. Overeaters have to learn a different behavior to deal with their compulsion. God gives these people the power to change their actions and takes away the defect, but they must cooperate with him.

Not all people familiar with the twelve-step program agree that we have to cooperate to remove shortcomings. Some argue that we don't play any part in removing character defects, except in asking God to remove them. To ask God to help, they say, and then to do it yourself is like telling someone to park your car, then grabbing the keys and parking it yourself. Proponents of this view argue that you have to let God do it all.

I question this attitude. If God really wants to do it all, then I dare anyone to go to the passenger side of their car, hold up the keys, and ask God to drive them to their destination. Wouldn't that be silly? God does-n't want to drive the car. God didn't create us so that he could take away all the fun or do all the work. He wants us to drive, but he wants to guide us. He wants to lead us in the right direction, along the best path, but he doesn't want to take over. God created us with the feeling of indepen-dence, the feeling of our own sense of power, the feeling of joy in living and acting as we please. He gave us these feelings so we can freely choose to allow his love to guide and touch us deeply, and then we, in turn, can freely touch others with his love as if it were our own. It is God's love and very life that affect us. But we make the choices; we perform the actions. By this means, we make that love and life our own.

Many Bible stories illustrate this principle of cooperating with God. In step three we talked about the story of Peter's walking on the water. Indeed, it was God's power holding Peter up and allowing him to walk on the stormy water, but Peter still had to walk. In the same way, it is God's power that holds us up when we call upon him during the storms we encounter, but we still have to walk—that is, overcome the difficulties by living the best we know.

Many people that Jesus or one of the prophets healed were told to get up and walk or to go and wash in a pool or in the Jordan River. These healings represent the spiritual healings God performs. If we want to be healed, we can't just sit and wait for miracles. We have to get up and get out of our state of disorder. We have to wash and be clean. Isn't that what the prophet's words mean: "Wash yourselves, make yourselves clean. . . . Put away the evil of your doings. . . . Though your sins be as scarlet they shall be as white as snow" (Isaiah 1:16–18). When Naaman, the Syrian leper, was told to go and wash in the Jordan River to be cleansed of his leprosy, it was, indeed, God who healed him; but Naaman still had to wash. If he hadn't performed the appropriate function, he would have remained diseased. In the same way, we have to wash symbolically; we have to put away our character defects as if the effort were ours alone while realizing at the same time that God actually removes them and heals us. God makes us whole.

ONE DEFECT AT A TIME

When we humbly ask God to remove our character defects, we should be specific. To begin this step, we need to find a quiet place to be alone, list our faults, and pray aloud for help. We may ask God to remove anger, stubbornness, self-pity, lust—every defect within ourselves. But after a general appeal, we select one or two defects that need special attention. We will work in cooperation with God to help rid us of these primary problems. After we make progress in these areas, we move on to one or two more shortcomings. We will continue this process throughout our lives, and as we remove each character defect, we will become better and more spiritual persons.

Why deal with one or two shortcomings at a time? Because we must focus on specifics if we really want God to remove defects. If we don't, we will be making a general plea to change without concentrating on what specifically needs changing. Besides, we are not capable of handling all character flaws at once. Let's face it; if we are honest in our inventory, we probably have a list of ten, twenty, or even thirty shortcomings. We simply can't focus on all of them simultaneously. It could be discouraging to focus on even four or five.

Imagine praying: "God, take away my anger, my stubbornness, my insecurity, my fears, my lusts, my envy, my insincerity, my hunger for power, my laziness, my self-pity, my this, my that." Why not just say, "God, take away my character defects. Thank you very much." A prayer like this would be useless. If we need only say, "God, take away my defects," then why take an inventory to discover these defects? The saying, "One day at a time" is apropos here if we change one word: "One defect at a time."

The defects an individual chooses to remove are a personal decision. At the outset, we may choose a defect or two that we can possibly remove with ease, or we might work at a bad habit or a fear. After removing these, we will be more confident and can advance to more difficult, deeply rooted character defects. On the other hand, we may initially choose to deal head-on with the defects that cause the most trouble. Perhaps we're at the end of our rope, dragged around by an inherent desire for pleasure or by a fiery temper that flares up to cause family suffering. These may be extremely difficult character defects to overcome, but we choose to tackle them first because they are the most destructive. Again, the choice is an individual one.

KEEPING OUR SPIRITS UP

When we begin the process of asking God to remove our defects of character, we may be surprised at how easily we shed some of them, never to see them again because they were minor and played an insignificant role in our lives. All we needed was a simple prayer to release them. Others, however, may be more difficult and put up a good fight. Don't be discouraged. Always bear in mind that we cannot expect spiritual perfection, only spiritual progress.

If God is really all-loving and all-powerful, why doesn't he remove all of these defects when we ask him? Why do some linger and continue to give trouble? They stay because we don't completely let go of them. Something inside us continues to hold on, and we have to work hard to discover what that something is. There can be a lot of pain before we recognize fully and completely that we are holding on to some defects that we really don't want to hold on to any longer.

God isn't going to take anything from us that we really haven't given up. Our freedom is important, both to God and to us. We may be holding on to some inner garbage; we ask God to take it from us, but when he reaches out to take it, we subconsciously pull away and clutch it close to our being. We are not ready to let it go. God is waiting to aid us, but we have to accept that aid.

Let's say a woman has a real problem with self-pity. Family pressures, problems at work, life in general release this "pity-me" posture. At times, she may acknowledge the self-pity to herself and to others. She even asks God to remove it from her—and her spirits lift. Life seems better, and it's fairly easy to appreciate all the good things around her and to concentrate more on her family or her tasks at work. Eventually, however, this inner feeling of self-pity resurfaces. This feeling is alluring. She toys with it and spends time counting her woes. At other times she rejects the feeling and makes an effort to forget about herself and get on with life. Nevertheless, it becomes more and more difficult to shrug off the self-pity until, finally, one day when things go wrong—her work load is heavy or she has had an argument with her spouse—she cries, "Why does God put me through all this? Why are people so rotten to me? What's the use?"

Why is the woman's character defect so tenacious? It is not because her life is pervasively evil or because God refuses to take her flaw from her. It is not because the defect is too powerful for her to handle. It remains a problem because she has difficulty letting it go completely. She prefers to feel sorry for herself again, to hold onto a part of the defect—and so it resurfaces in full form. It will continue to recur until she wholeheartedly decides to let go.

The story of a good friend of mine—a recovering alcoholic—illustrates this point. He had tried many, many times to stop drinking but just couldn't seem to do it. He'd get help and get sober. Then, one night or another, he'd be feeling safe, even adventurous, and head off to a friend's party or a card game with the boys. As he drove to his friend's house, he would pray, "Please, God, help me not to drink. Please help me not to drink." But it never worked. He'd arrive there and eventually get loaded.

Not until his third attempt did he finally lick the problem. He was taking the usual course; but as he approached his friend's house, he started thinking about what he was doing. He soon felt his powerlessness over the situation. He didn't want to drink that night, but he didn't know how he could stop himself. In desperation he prayed aloud, "God, don't just help me not to drink. Make me so I won't drink! Please make me stop." A voice from within responded immediately. It said quite strongly, "Turn the car around! Turn it around right now!" And he felt the power to do that. He turned the car around and went home. Today, he avoids these parties at all costs and has been sober for about two years.

Obviously, my friend should have known he couldn't associate with the same old crowd. But look deeper into the problem. In the beginning, attempting to stay sober, he never really turned the problem over to God. He'd ask God to help, but he wouldn't let God in. God had not been silent on this issue nor did he refuse to deal with the man until he begged for help. God was there each time my friend headed toward another party, saying quite strongly, "Turn the car around." But my friend wasn't listening. It was only when he felt complete powerlessness over the situation and let go that he heard God's voice and allowed God's power to give him the strength to turn around and go home. Finally, he became enlightened. My friend realized that within his desire to go to these parties was hidden a desire to keep drinking. He hadn't really let it go until he reached that final state of desperation and prayed to God not only to help him but also to make him stop.

So it is with any of us. It will not always be easy to allow God to remove our character defects, but, at those times when we wonder why God has not taken them away, we must take a good, hard look at ourselves. What are we holding onto? Every time we resist one defect, we make progress. Eventually, when we are freed from them all, we will be blessed with a new life.

A NEW LIFE

We do make real progress. Even those character defects that seemed to manipulate and ruin our lives are taken away. We may have struggled for years with certain fears; but after surrendering the fears to God, we will find that they are gone and the discomfort in the stomach or chest is no more. We are healed! Anger, resentment, and jealousy may have plagued us. It is a tough battle, but after a time we learn to relinquish the hold on those negative feelings and our lives change. We no longer get angry; the resentment or jealousy is replaced with concern for others as well as a genuine belief in ourselves and our own worth. Old habits that may have seemed impossible to eradicate vanish once we've learned to turn them over to God. Truly, a new life has begun.

That is the last part of this step—to begin a new life. As we allow God, with our cooperation, to remove our shortcomings, he opens up a new life for us. We have to be willing to start again in all facets of our lives and to leave the past behind. In this step, we let go not only of our character defects but also of our past life and our memories. We start anew.

Perhaps we had an unhappy childhood; memories may still be affecting our view of life. Perhaps we suffer from guilt and find it difficult to forget something we did five, ten, even fifteen years ago. We carry that baggage around in an attempt to make up for past mistakes. Let go! Take responsibility for the wrongs, right them as much as you can, and make amends wherever possible. But don't carry the guilt. Forget the past; begin a new life. In Matthew 8:22, Jesus says, "Let the dead bury their dead." The past is dead. We are who we are *now* and won't be the same person even tomorrow. We must be reborn completely. Think about it. Say to yourself, "Nothing in the past has to affect me. I am not the person I used to be; I can begin again. I can be born anew. I can live for the first time—really live!" As Swedenborg says in *Arcana Coelestia*, ¶18, "The old person must die before the new one can be conceived."

The more we work step seven the more we grow spiritually into a new life and new healing. Like a lame man who leaves his bed and walks, we too can leave our infirmity behind and walk in ways of happiness and peace. Like a blind woman who receives sight, we will behold the true beauty of this world, not just in nature but in relationships, in the face of a friend and in a child's smile. We may have been deaf to inner guidance, but now we hear a gentle voice within, leading us, guiding us, and comforting us with tender care. Like a leper healed of his numbing disease, we begin to sense the joy of life. Inner numbness departs. Emotions well up within us that may be hard to control. Nevertheless, we feel vibrant, inwardly clean, and called forth to a new life. The old person has died; we are now born anew!

EXERCISES FOR STEP SEVEN

Allowing improvements

1. Pick one shortcoming you've been thinking about. Ask God to remove it, then stop enacting this flaw as if you had the capacity to do it on your own. What happens? Is this easier than when you did this same thing in step three? If it is easier, why is it so? If not, why not?

2. When you suspect you are in a negative state, notice the enjoyment you may be having from it. What is the payoff for the negative state? What negative delight is blocking higher enjoyment? Let go of the negative and allow the positive to take its place.

Step Eight

Made a list of all persons we had harmed and became willing to make amends to all

THE NEED FOR THIS STEP is evident in a twelve-step program for the recovering alcoholic. Anyone alcoholism has affected knows the damage that comes from this disease. The alcoholic might have harmed many people, and so needs to make amends. But the basic principles in this step are important for anyone wanting spiritual growth. We may have many names on the list of persons we've injured, while others may not have any. Most of us, however, can bring to mind a few people we have harmed in one way or another and can right wrongs and make amends.

This step dovetails with step seven. Making a list of the people we have harmed and then making amends help us to clear the slate, dump the guilt, and begin a new life. Who have we hurt in the past? Possibly we lashed out at someone with cruel words or accusations. Or in a selfish way we cheated someone and now regret it. Maybe we actually hurt someone physically by accident—but we've never resolved the guilt. Memories can haunt us and cling to us like leeches. If it is possible to right the wrongs, then we have golden opportunities to repair the damage and let go of the guilt. With a clear conscience, we can work toward a useful and constructive life that lets us see ourselves and our relationships with others in a new light.

Making amends also helps us turn good intentions into action and dreams into reality. Heretofore, we have focused on ourselves. This, of course, is good and necessary because it's important to get our own act together before we can change our attitude toward others. Now we reach the point where we change our focus from looking inward to looking outward.

It's possible that we become so wrapped up and concerned with our own spiritual growth that we forget other people. Imagine saying to someone, "Will you stop bothering me? I'm too busy trying to be a spiritual person to be concerned with you right now." Of course, we wouldn't say that, but we can feel that way at times. In an attempt to feel good and more spiritual, we remove ourselves from the real world, from the needs of others. Also, in working the first seven steps, we will experience great joy at the changes taking place within. Our enthusiasm to continue the quest may cause loved ones to feel left behind and perplexed at our behavior. If this happens, we've missed the point in our quest for spirituality.

Making a list of those we have injured brings us back to reality. It's a reminder that we have some past hurts that need mending. It forces us to show concern for others. When we list the names of people we have harmed, what we have done to them, and how to make amends, we begin to see how we affect other people. We see the harm we have caused but also recognize the potential for good we can have on others. We create the opportunity to live constructively instead of destructively. We rebuild for ourselves and others the bridges we had wrecked in the past. We cross those bridges and look into the hearts of others, concerned with their concerns. We begin to love and to bring that love into life.

CODEPENDENCY

Step eight helps us build relationships. But often some of our past relationships need to be reordered before they can be rebuilt. A codependent is a person who is addicted to a sick relationship, much like an alcoholic is addicted to alcohol. People who suffer from codependency often come from dysfunctional families. The spouse of an alcoholic may often be as sick as, even sicker than, the alcoholic. The root of the problem may lie in the alcoholism, but the spouse living with the diseased person for years may subconsciously learn sick patterns of thought and behavior that not only enable the alcoholic but also give the codependent a "fix."

A good example of this is the wife (or the husband) of an alcoholic who finds herself completely wrapped up in her husband's addiction. She sets herself up as the caretaker in the relationship, making sure others do not discover her husband's disease. She lies to his boss with the excuse that her husband is sick, when actually he is hung over. She cleans up after his drunken excursions, supports his denials, and may even become his supplier by keeping alcohol in the home.

Surprisingly, the wife can detest the alcoholism yet continue to enable it. In these situations, the wife plays the martyr. Certainly, she carries the burden of the entire family, of home management, and of financial responsibilities; but her sense of self is built upon this burden. Frequently, she becomes obsessed with her husband's addiction. He becomes the target of her anger and resentment, yet her sense of security hinges on his behavior; this is the world as she has come to know it, and she has established a modicum of control over it. She becomes addicted to the status quo, to the point of feeling self-important because she is the caretaker. She is addicted to the sick relationship.

It is not unusual, then, that marriages of many alcoholics end in divorce, not while the alcoholic is drinking but after the person gets help. Working through the twelve-step program of AA, the husband wakes up spiritually, wants to assume those responsibilities he had abandoned. He finds he is not as dependent on his spouse as he once was and is ready to start again. Many times the wife can't tolerate this change. She has become so addicted to the sick relationship, so used to being in charge, that her distorted sense of self-esteem is thrown into turmoil because of his new sobriety. That is why Al-Anon was created. It not only helps those who live with a problem drinker but also helps those who live with a recovering alcoholic learn to recover themselves.

Codependency is not exclusive to alcoholism, although it most often shows itself in that disease. Many other people find themselves in sick relationships. They put all their sense of self-worth into what others think about them and how others treat them. Some people find themselves addicted to abusive relationships, whether the abuse is emotional, physical, or even spiritual.

In *True Christian Religion*, ¶448, Swedenborg talks about such fused relationships and how detrimental they can be to people. He says that those who have such codependent relationships

> *cannot be separated like others in accordance with order . . . for they are bound together interiorly as to the spirit, nor can they be torn apart, because they are like scions ingrafted into branches; consequently, if one . . . is in heaven and the other . . . in hell, they stick together much as a sheep tied to a wolf, or a goose to a fox, or a dove to a hawk. . . . [T]he good spirit suffers severely.*

Making amends does not mean continuing to be a codependent nor does it mean turning the other cheek and becoming a slave to another's approval, behavior, addictive personality, or character disorder. Now and then, making amends means simply saying "No!"

The purpose of steps eight and nine is to right the wrong and begin anew in relationships. Often, righting a wrong takes only a kind heart to accomplish reconciliation. Yet righting wrongs can also mean escaping a sick relationship by relying on your own initiative, learning to be your own person, and showing love and compassion to others. A wife who stops enabling her alcoholic husband is showing him far more love than one who fulfills his every whim. A man who terminates an unhealthy dependence on a woman is expressing more love for her than by remaining in the sick relationship and allowing her to use him. Sick relationships need not be broken and abandoned; they do, however, need to be rebuilt. It may be necessary to show tough love for a while and to separate long enough to find independence—and true love.

When I went to a twelve-step group for codependents the first time, a woman who was introducing newcomers to the program told her story. It is a good illustration of the points above.

She had been in a sick relationship with her husband for over twenty years. Her marriage was always in turmoil because she was completely wrapped up in her husband's behavior, obsessed with his actions to the point of preparing for divorce. It wasn't until he was diagnosed as having a terminal disease that she felt she must turn somewhere for help to cope with him under these new and stressful circumstances. When she understood the nature of codependency and learned to separate herself from her spouse, she began to love him. Before that time, she had focused her attention on his problems because she was afraid to face her own. After learning about codependency, she began to face her own needs and to break away from the sick dependence she had on her husband. She held her ground and demanded dignity and respect from him. "As I began to see myself for what I really was, no longer dependent on my husband for happiness," she said, "I began to truly love him and to care for him in his condition. . . . We are lovers now, not necessarily in a physical sense, but deep within. He always thought he loved me, but I know that not until now did I really love him—and in a healthy way. I am not going to divorce him. I want to make his last days as warm and loving as possible."

When we reflect on the relationships we have built—the people we affect deeply and those who deeply affect us—we should look for those we have harmed and be willing to make amends. But we also should look for those relationships that harm us, be willing to break them down, and rebuild them. This is loving—a loving that leads to good and healthy relationships.

MAKING A LIST

How do we complete step eight? First, we should set aside a block of time to reflect on our relationships, on our misdeeds, and on those we have harmed. Next, we make a list of these relationships, misdeeds, injured persons, and add an idea or two on how to make amends. It's a good idea to keep the list nearby for a few days in case additions to the list come to mind. When the list is completed, we are ready for action.

We must be willing to make amends to *all*. This takes courage. We can easily approach some people and right the wrongs we have done them. Others, however, we may have vowed never to see again. Similarly, we can atone for some of our bad deeds without much of a problem, but others may cause real shame and embarrassment. Nevertheless, we have to deal with them if we want to bury the past and begin a new life. That this process may be a long and difficult task is inconsequential; the task is a necessity.

This step demands a great deal of reflection on the reason we should make amends and the best time and way to accomplish our ends. Sometimes immediate action is the best way. We must simply say to ourselves, "I'm scared to death, but I will do this." Then we jump in and do our best.

Have you ever had the experience of being really hot and then had the opportunity to jump into a cool, refreshing pool or lake? The cold water will be welcome but you still hesitate because of the initial shock. If you delay too long, you may never take the plunge and enjoy the water. The best thing to do is simply to jump. Some people rub water on their bodies and their heads and go through a slow process of getting used to the cold. Even that is better than standing in the boiling heat, thinking how much you'd like to be refreshed, but anxiously holding back because of the first few cold and uncomfortable seconds.

A willingness to make amends is much the same. You'll feel refreshed when you have completed your mission, but if you hesitate too long and concentrate on the moments of initial discomfort, you'll never do it. So it's best to simply jump in. The outcome is worth it.

EXERCISES FOR STEP EIGHT

Beginning that list

1. Make a list of five people you have harmed.

2. Write down an idea or two about how you might best make amends.

Step Nine

Began to make amends, to do good, to be honest and faithful in all our affairs, and to walk humbly with our God

WHEN WE ACTUALLY BEGIN to make amends to those we have harmed, our primary goal is reconciliation. That is, we resolve the wrongs and the ill will, and mend the broken relationships. With reconciliation, we leave the past and start life and relationships anew in a productive manner.

Amends may be as simple as a sincere apology via a visit, a phone call, or a letter. Circumstances govern the approach. The first time I took step nine, I gave a verbal apology to one person and a written one to another.

About six months before coming into contact with the twelve steps, I had lied to an associate who questioned me about a group of teenage kids who were drinking in the park. Their drinking was especially disturbing to the teacher since he had cautioned them about teenage drinking. I wasn't actually with the group, but I had talked to them for about fifteen minutes the night they were in the park. Weak-kneed, I told my associate I hadn't seen anyone. Why? Possibly because I didn't want to implicate anyone or maybe it was just easier to stay out of it. Regardless, he returned to my office later and said, "If you didn't see the kids, why did they say they saw you and spent some time talking with you?" Flushed from embarrassment, I mumbled something but stuck to my story.

As I was taking my ninth step six months later, I walked into his office and told him the truth. Indeed, I had lied. I apologized for such a stupid move and asked him to forgive me. He laughed and started recounting stupid things he had done as a teacher. We are now good friends.

My other apology was in a letter. I have yet to talk about my misdeed face to face with this person. We were good friends when I was in college and theological school. That was before I learned about the twelve steps, and I had some serious problems: I saw life in two colors—black and white—and two ways—right and wrong. My friend made a few ethical mistakes, mistakes that anyone can make from time to time. But as a young, idealistic, not too realistic or compassionate theological student, I saw only the wrong. When my friend faltered, I got out the cannon and fired the big one. I called the person evil, selfish, a devil, a mere semblance of a human being, and more! I cut all ties and walked away. Believe me, it made an impression.

It took almost five years and a move eight hundred miles away before I finally wrote a short letter of apology saying simply that I was wrong and that I hoped my friend would forgive me. I have not received a reply to that letter, but I don't deserve one. That is not the focus of this step. The focus lies in my attempt to right the wrong, clear the slate, and start again. And I feel better about it. I know that I am forgiven—at least by God and myself.

Sometimes making amends does not center on apology and reconciliation. It may require repayment for a debt or anonymously doing a good deed for someone. There is great opportunity for creativity in this step, but we must be sincere, actually right the wrong, and make amends in the best way possible.

At one time you may have dipped into your company's expense account. Now you have the company on your list for making amends. Obviously, you don't want to walk into the boss's office and apologize for ripping off the company for the last twelve years. But you can make amends by replacing the money in a petty cash fund available to you without being obvious about it. Use your creativity. Deliver mysterious envelopes containing cash donations to your boss's desk. Work overtime without remuneration. You can usually find ways to make amends without being noticed.

There are times when, for good reasons, a person wants anonymity. For example, it would be imprudent—even destructive—to tell someone about an affair you had with their spouse years ago. What good would such a confession do? To make amends in this and similar circumstances is meant to fix the wrong, not to ruin another person's life simply to make yourself feel better. Make amends only when the action would not harm self or others.

Use good judgment in making amends. Seriously consider the best way to go about it and be completely honest about the motives for making amends. By apologizing, do we hope for an apology from the person we are in discord with? Are we making an appointment to see that person under the pretense of making an apology when we are actually planning to lay out all our resentments and unload on him or her? It's easy to do. We may say something like, "I'm really sorry I left you and the kids, but you were a real witch. I'm sure you're a lot different now," or "I'm sorry I didn't pay back the loan, but at the time I thought you were one of the stingiest people I'd ever known." That is not employing the ninth step correctly. We make amends to take away the negative, concentrate on the positive, and come to reconciliation. Most of the time the only words we need are, "I'm sorry." They may not say it all, but often they say enough.

LIFE IS MORE THAN APOLOGIES

People familiar with the original twelve steps of AA will recognize that this step reads differently from the original. For spiritual recovery, step nine says, "We have begun to make amends, to do good, to be honest and faithful in all our affairs, and to walk humbly with our God." AA's ninth step says, "We made direct amends to such people wherever possible, except when to do so would injure them or others." For some who belong to AA, changing this or any step might seem as unthinkable as altering the Ten Commandments. But keep in mind that the twelve steps were designed originally and specifically to help the recovering alcoholic. They were not designed for everyone. The twelve steps to spiritual recovery, however, are meant for all.

The spiritual life is more than a life of apologies. It is more than recounting repeatedly what a terrible person we've been and how much better we now are. The spiritual life is a positive life in which we cease hurting others, make amends, and go forward to a life of goodness, honesty, joy, and love. That is why step nine of the twelve steps for spiritual growth tells us to go forward in life and "do good, be honest and faithful in all our affairs, and walk humbly with our God." It launches us into the full and satisfying life that is readily available.

Helping people, showing love, doing good and unselfish deeds bring joy. When we learn to love others, we are blessed with all that is meaningful, fulfilling, and beautiful. Goodness and happiness are synonymous.

In Luke 6:38, Jesus says, "Give and it will be given unto you." This doesn't mean that if we put out money now, we'll cash in on some great reward in heaven. Jesus also said, "The Kingdom of God is within you." I strongly believe in the concept of heaven, but we begin to build that heaven within ourselves here on earth. Swedenborg says that we make our lives a heaven or a hell right now, by our actions, our thoughts, our feelings. The reward of a good life is the sheer joy that it brings. Essentially, that is what heaven is all about: goodness, love, happiness, and joy. Why wait? We can have that here to the degree that we give.

Think about a special time in your life when your whole being was filled with joy, if only for a brief moment. What was at the core of the experience? It was love, the desire to be close to another; love, the flame that warms another; love, the magnetic force that pulls us closer to another human being in an effort to become one; love, the force within that does good without thought of reward. Love gives hope and love brings joy.

Most parents try to make their children's lives happy lives. In my relationship with my children, I am attuned to their ups and downs and try to strengthen their good feelings and alleviate the bad ones. I observe their state of happiness and discover that they are happiest when they express love, when they are giving, not receiving or taking. No one can quickly forget the face of a child who has made some special gift for another child. It beams with joy. When one child helps another child find his way or consoles her after a fall, a spirit of joy pervades both children. Parents too experience the same kind of joy when they observe this gift of joy in their children. Parents rejoice when their child takes those first steps, says those first words, or brings home a prize from school for a job well done. Parents rejoice as their children grow into young men and women who learn to think and act for themselves. There is, of course, a lot of pain in parenting. Nevertheless, the joy and pain merge into love to make it all worthwhile.

After we make amends, we go forth with new hearts on a journey of love. An adventure lies before us, and we experience a transformation of character. We find self-worth, contentment, companionship, and warmth. The journey is smooth. We keep a cool head, do good wherever we can, live honestly, do our job faithfully, and walk hand in hand with God.

The spiritual life is not a complicated or grandiose scheme. We take life one day at a time, one obstacle at a time, one achievement at a time. That is the reason that step nine indicates that we are trying to act honestly and faithfully in our dealings with others and to be humble. If we keep a clear conscience and contain our ego, we will make progress. We won't set our expectations too high. We won't fill ourselves with guilt or remorse over failures or fill ourselves with pride and conceit over victories. God leads us every step of the way. If we remain humble, do the best we can, and hold God's hand, we will never be lost; we'll keep marching down that path toward spiritual success and prosperity.

I end this chapter with another quotation from *True Christian Religion*, ¶484, where Swedenborg makes the process a simple one with great promise:

> *My friend, shun evil and do good and believe in the Lord with all your heart and in all your soul, and the Lord will love you, and will give you a love of doing [what is good] and faith to believe. Then from love you will do good, and from faith, which is trust, you will believe; and if you persevere in so doing, a mutual union will be*

effected [between you and God], which will be perpetual; and this is salvation itself and eternal life.

EXERCISES FOR STEP NINE

....

Working toward forgiveness and reconciliation

1. Select a person you have harmed in a small way; make amends verbally, openly, or covertly.

2. When a person offends you, ask God to forgive you for an offense against another. Place them side by side and note the difference. "Forgive us our trespasses as we forgive those who trespass against us."

3. When you feel regret or anxiety, observe a connection with the past. Let go and recall something positive in the here and now. Say to yourself, "This present moment is eternity; I am in the perfect place at the perfect time."

Step Ten

Continued to take personal inventory and when we were wrong promptly admitted it

STEP TEN IS THE first step of the twelve that indicates that spiritual growth and change are a process. Each day we move along the path we have chosen. We continue with the personal inventory, keeping an eye on ourselves and our spiritual growth. We maintain a clear conscience and an open mind. And thus we continue to grow.

This is important. Some people believe that spiritual change and growth happen instantaneously, that there is not a progression. They think that confessing belief in a set of teachings automatically achieves spirituality. Granted, there may be a time when one "sees the light" and begins a conversion, but the battle for spiritual growth is not over. It has just begun. Yes, God forgives all; but if a person is unwilling to accept that forgiveness by a change in lifestyle, then that forgiveness doesn't accomplish anything.

It may be comforting to think that with a confession of belief we don't have to change, work, or grow. But, of course, this is a false notion because character flaws don't disappear simply because we utter a profession of faith. How easy it would be to say a few magic words that would—presto!—change us into spiritual people. But not life, not human nature, not God work that way. Becoming a spiritual person is a lifelong process through day-by-day growth. We claim only spiritual progress, not spiritual perfection. Reality is hard to face. Our human nature doesn't want to deal with problems, but the sooner we confront them, the sooner we will know a genuine and fulfilling spirituality.

OLD WAYS SOMETIMES RETURN

Step ten cultivates being aware of life rather than hiding from it. This day-by-day step advises us to keep eyes open to our spiritual growth and to recognize when old habits may be creeping back in. Steps one through nine help us recognize and remove destructive tendencies; step ten makes sure they don't become an active force once again.

Some old tendencies, though, do come back. In working the previous steps, we turn things over to God, start a new life, and make great spiritual strides and changes. We find, however, that bad habits and ways of thinking—once banished—do at times raise their ugly heads.

For instance, we might have let go of anger or resentment. Six months, maybe a year or two have passed and we haven't lost our temper or felt resentful. Then one day a co-worker really tests our patience. Perhaps we are teaching a man to do a job, and he keeps making the same mistake or fools around and wastes time. Anger flares up, and we scold him for his ineptitude. Later, we ask ourselves, "Whoa, where did that come from? I thought I was rid of that."

These destructive tendencies can also resurface more subtly. We might have been quite the egotist, but the twelve steps helped to bring about a much more balanced, humble human being. Consequently, life in general has improved. When this happens, we may gradually forget about a higher power and attribute our successes and triumphs to the fruit of our own labor and ignore the benefits of following a higher power. We may take the credit for the good things we've accomplished in life and give little credit to God. Slowly the egotism begins to emerge, and we are again full of self and our own sense of importance, right where we started with this character defect.

Why do these destructive tendencies come back? Can we ever be rid of them completely? The answer, of course, is that we never eradicate them completely. Like peeling an onion, we do away with one layer at a time. Sometimes we can get the feeling that the layers will never end. But each time we deal with them we take away some of their power and effect on our lives so that we can change dramatically for the better. By working the twelve steps—especially step ten—these character defects can eventually be reduced to a size where they are, for all practical purposes, ineffectual.

An elderly woman once told me she had been working with this program for years. She was ninety-one years old, a sweet, angelic lady. When I asked her if she had always been so sweet, her reply surprised me. She said, "Sometimes I feel I've been working on the same shortcomings all of my life. I don't see much progress—only the same old problems."

How depressing! Had she really been working on these same problems all of her life? Had she made no progress? Everyone acquainted with her knew she had grown in her love, her charm, and her spirituality. Everyone could sense this, even in a first meeting with her. However, she herself was unaware that her spiritual labors were not in vain but actually quite fruitful. She had grown dramatically, but a perception of her personal shortcomings increased with that growth. Being so aware of them, she did not see the progress she had indeed made over them. This can happen to anyone who focuses on and struggles with character defects.

There are times when we need to take a good look at ourselves to see these changes. If we feel dismayed over our shortcomings, it is a signal to reflect on what life was like before we began our journey toward spiritual growth. It won't take long to recognize progress.

To illustrate, compare our spiritual program—the cleansing of character—to window washing. The windows are dirty and so badly smudged that we can hardly see through them. Before beginning the program, we seemed to have little control over the situation. The dirty windows were bothersome; they blocked out the sunlight, but we had little initiative to wash them. There were too many and they were just too dirty.

Then begins our program for spiritual growth. We call on a greater power to motivate us and to start on one window at a time. The room seems brighter with each washing. There are still a few smudges, though, that just don't seem to come off. We spend hours working to remove them. These few smudges trouble us a great deal. We focus on them, even become dismayed over them. If only we could get rid of these smudges, the windows would be clean. We say, "I've been washing windows all of my life, but this dirt is still here!"

How quickly we forget. Once the room was dark and gloomy; now it is full of light. While it seems we have been doing the same job all along, things really have changed. Once, we felt powerless over the dirt, and we sat in the dark. Now light pours in, but we become concerned and weary over a few remaining marks on the pane. Again, we must step back and appraise our work. Yes, we have changed and grown; most of our personal dirt has been removed. We must simply recognize this fact and accept that no human being is perfect.

The emergence of a particular shortcoming does not indicate a sign of spiritual digression nor does it mean we are faltering or going backward in our spiritual journey. Some shortcomings come back, so we can deal with them on a deeper level.

Let's return to the garden analogy. The first time we deal with a specific shortcoming we merely chop off its head like a weed in the garden. The next time it appears, we cut it off at ground level. The third time it emerges we decide, "I'll get on my knees and dig the darn thing out." It disappears forever.

If the first time we faced that shortcoming we could see how ugly it really is, we'd be horrified. God lets us see only a little so we won't be afraid to tackle just a bit at a time. Had we seen the entire malignant problem immediately, we'd have said, "Why try? It's too much for me."

When you become dismayed about your spiritual growth because a shortcoming recurs, ask this simple question: "How do I feel about this?" Think about a character defect you may have suffered from—egotism, resentment, or even an addiction of some sort. If you are now concerned about it and see it as an enemy rather than a friend, then you have come a long way. Before you started down your spiritual path, how did you feel about that shortcoming? You loved it; it was part of you. You loved being an egotist. You loved being resentful of other people. You loved the high of alcohol or drugs. These things were killing you, but they ruled your life. Now they no longer rule you. You don't love them anymore. When they do come up, they become an intruder to be dismissed immediately. You've come a long way in your effort to change, and you are a radically different person.

PERSONAL INVENTORY

Step ten allows us to continue on the path of change and growth. Continuing with a personal inventory makes it possible to detect destructive forces before they once again become active. By observing our behavior on a regular basis and getting to know ourselves better, we can, for example, see the potential for anger coming back or the egotism before it becomes a ruling factor in our lives once again. Seeing these tendencies begin to surface, we can deal with them before they cause trouble. Like weeds growing in a garden, we nip them in the bud.

This personal inventory acts as a shield against the emergence of destructive tendencies. When we tend to be stubborn, angry, or selfish, we anticipate these feelings and can fend off their influence. Perhaps a voice from within tells us to retaliate, or to take what is not rightfully ours, or to find fault. By working step ten, we can stop and say to ourselves, "No! I'm not getting back into that trap." These enemy attacks don't breach our defenses anymore, and we remain spiritually healthy.

The protective shield that step ten creates works in our exterior lives as well as in our interior lives. People don't affect us in the same way they once did. Who hasn't experienced a friend or relative who seems to delight in trying to upset us? Say that you have a problem with one of your children. Your friend may ask, "How's your son doing these days? Is he still giving you trouble? Your heart must tighten when the phone rings at night." You know what I'm talking about. Whatever your problem—disciplining the children, marital woes, overeating, even a blemish on your nose—these "button pushers" will be sure to exploit it and do their best to kindle your fire.

This step acts as a buffer to these destructive exterior voices also. When they attempt to push our buttons, we don't react. By learning to deflect their statements, we save ourselves from the destructive forces they enkindle and expose their own malice. Their vicious attacks suggest that the problem lies within the attacker. After attempting to push the same buttons without results, they may give up and see others who don't have this remarkable shield.

ADMITTING MISTAKES

Because we are not saints, it is quite probable that some shortcomings may slip by the shield to result in foolish mistakes. This is normal in spiritual growth. The key is to recognize the destructive force and to deal with it immediately. Step ten emphasizes the necessity to admit promptly that we are wrong.

Human nature is prone to make excuses for mistakes, but every excuse allows the shortcoming to live on in us. Admitting when we are wrong is essential for spiritual growth. Denial is half the problem of alcoholism or drug addiction. Just as a personal inventory acts as a shield to preserve health, denial acts as a shield to preserve sickness. Every excuse is one more blanket covering the problem. Every denial is one more step away from spiritual growth and a step into the quicksand of an unmanageable life.

By promptly admitting wrongs, we refuse to allow destructive tendencies a haven in our active lives. Our shortcoming may surface from time to time, but, by admitting we have been wrong, we let go of that shortcoming. For instance, when our ego rises and we do or say something harmful, we admit, "That was my fault. The old ego got in the way again, I'm sorry." That phrase—"I'm sorry"—will deflate the most inflated ego. The ego shrinks and whimpers away to the recesses of our mind; we become humble, healthy, and balanced human beings.

Step ten is a shield and defender of our spiritual lives. With an open eye on ourselves and our spiritual development, we see our spiritual enemies—our destructive tendencies—before they attack and overwhelm us. By working step ten, nothing will stop us from attaining and keeping a happy life. Understandably, there will be ups and downs; but a good attitude, coupled with following the program, assures that the ups will be long and high and the downs just a stumble now and then as we walk the path of spiritual life.

EXERCISES FOR STEP TEN

Building up strong defenses

1. When you feel upset by a thing, a situation, or a person, remember that upsets do not come from an outside source but from within; observe your reactions to the situation from that point of view.

2. When you have a negative thought about another person, focus on a positive trait about that person. Do this when new negative thoughts arise.

Step Eleven

Sought through prayer and meditation to improve our conscious contact with God as we understood him, praying only for knowledge of his will for us and the power to carry that out

IT IS GOOD that there are many different ways of praying and understanding what prayer accomplishes. Variety is the spice of spiritual life much as it is for everyday worldly life. This is also true in the way we go about praying. Each person must have a philosophy and style of prayer. This is not to say that some prayers aren't more conducive to spiritual growth than others. People can abuse prayer rather than use it.

How often have we heard someone say, "Pray for me." Perhaps we use that line ourselves. Praying for others is commendable; but, in asking others for prayers, we should be wary that we might be using this as a way of shirking our own responsibilities. It is comforting to know that someone is remembering us in prayer as we move through a particularly difficult situation; but if we find ourselves often asking others to pray for us, we might question our motives. Are we hoping that, through the prayers of others, the right things will happen without any effort on our part?

Our spiritual growth cannot depend only on the prayers of others. It is easy to ask someone to pray that we make the right choices for a more spiritual and happy life but at the same time never personally make an effort toward living that spiritual life. The knowledge that others care for our well-being and support our efforts at change can help us to achieve our goals, but their support and care cannot get us to the end. Only our own efforts can do that.

I knew a young man who asked me regularly to pray for him to lead a better life. His certainly seemed out of control. Day after day, week after week, year after year, he'd come to my office and complain about his miserable life and the many mistakes he'd made; he'd insist that he wanted to be a better person. He'd always say, "Pray for me, Reverend; pray that I'll get my life together." Then he'd exit the office and slip back into his same lifestyle. When his guilt became too much for him to handle, he'd show up again to dump it on my desk and ask for my prayers. One time he pleaded, "Reverend, pray for me; pray that someone comes along and gives me a kick in the pants to get me going the right way." After working with this man for years, I agreed that a kick in the pants would do him more good than any of my prayers. He wasn't willing to help himself; his pleas for my prayers were for his own convenience, to make him feel better because he was too spiritually lazy to take care of himself.

Another deficient type of prayer we might practice from time to time is the "foxhole prayer," based on the familiar saying that originated during World War II: there are no atheists in the foxhole. In this scenario, even the most irreligious person will turn to God in times of trouble and say, "Please God, I'll do anything you want if you get me out of this. I'll turn over a new leaf! I'll change my life! Just help me now."

Everyone has used this kind of prayer in a jam. We can follow our destructive tendencies into all sorts of situations with little thought of God until we back ourselves against the wall. Suddenly, God becomes our best friend; we pray for forgiveness and pledge our entire lives to him.

But it doesn't work. God has already forgiven us for the wrongs we've done. But if we don't open our hearts to him, we don't accept his forgiveness. What happens, then, when we get out of our current jam? If God was not in our life before this difficulty, then we almost always leave him behind once we are extricated from our problem. We might even forget to thank God. We're the same people; prayers motivated by fear are not going to change us. When the fear disappears, the prayers—and God— disappear. He doesn't leave us; *we leave him.* Spiritual change takes place only when we freely make choices and use the gift of reason God gave us.

Bargaining with God is another abuse of prayer. We say, "God, just give me this one thing and I'll change. I really will! I'll be kinder to the kids; I'll be faithful to my spouse; I'll be more considerate at work. If you do this for me, I'll go to church every Sunday!"

Have you ever heard this prayer: "Just let me win the lottery, God, and I'll give fifty percent of it to the church"? Have you used it? Can you imagine God saying, "Hmmm, I'll tell you what. Give me seventy-five percent, Bud, and you've got a deal."

Let's use our heads when it comes to prayer. God is not Santa Claus in the sky who listens to our list of wants and then drops them to us down the chimney. He is not an indulgent or negligent parent who happens to be in charge of the human race, sitting in heaven wondering what to do. If we pray hard enough or get others to pray, a light doesn't suddenly come on causing God to grant our wishes. It's the sincerity of the prayer, not the magnitude, volume, or variety that counts.

Sometimes people adopt these faulty notions of God. After all, they reason, if God is really all-knowing, he knows what we need before we ask. They can even quote Mark 6:8, where Jesus says, "Your Father knows the things you need before you ask him." Sure God knows; that's not in question. Our willing acknowledgment and cooperation are needed to let in his help.

THE BEST PRAYERS

Of course, it's good to pray for others and to have others pray for us. It is good to pray to God in times of need. In such prayers we acknowledge the power greater than ourselves and the source of all good. But if prayers are abused or misapplied, they will have little or nothing to do with our spiritual lives and our relationship with God. If we use only "earthly" prayers, then we remain earthly people, stuck on the natural plane of life.

The best prayers—those with lasting effect that bring about real change and happiness—are the prayers that center on our spiritual life, that seek God's will for us, not our will for God, and the power to carry out God's will. That's what Jesus meant when he says in Matthew 6:33,

"Seek first the kingdom of God and his righteousness and all these things shall be added unto you."

God may not always answer our earthly prayers. We may pray hard for a new car, but God knows if we get that car we will drive it too fast around the local "dead man's curve" and kill ourselves. We may pray for a more loving, caring spouse, but God doesn't change anyone into a more loving person without that person's consent. God may not always be able to give us what we want, but he gives us what we need. This is good.

In our spiritual lives and prayers for spiritual growth, God can and does give what we truly want and need. When we pray for hope, God gives hope. When we pray for strength, God gives strength. When we pray for a loving heart, God gives us a loving heart. Why? Because these prayers open the door and allow God to come in. The spiritual changes may take time, according to our willingness to accept God's help through prayer and effort. But when that happens, God is there to make necessary changes.

God stands at the door ready to enter and bless us with the treasures of a spiritual life. Our prayers to live in harmony with God's ways open that door. Prayers having to do with our spiritual welfare are not a magic formula so much as a therapeutic process toward deeper spirituality. Prayers do not cause God to reach out his hand; rather, they put our hands in God's hand—which is always there for us.

Why do we ask God for knowledge of his will and the power to carry it out? For one reason, our life becomes simpler. We don't have to carry the world on our shoulders, manipulate people, or change events. We let God take care of the world. Also, we let go of selfishness through this kind of prayer. We start asking God for what we need, not for what we desire, which may be nothing more than a transitory whim.

With this prayerful attitude, a feeling of peace comes over us. Not only are we at ease because we allow God to direct our lives, but we move into the gentle stream of his providence. When we pray for God's guidance, we allow him to draw us toward the right path, the one that leads to true happiness and deep spirituality.

Prayer should be a fundamental part of our spiritual lives, but it does not always come naturally. If you do not pray regularly, try reciting the Lord's Prayer or the twenty-third psalm occasionally. These are particularly helpful in times of need or crisis or meditative reflection. The Serenity Prayer is a part of many twelve-step programs: "God, grant me the serenity to accept the things I cannot change, courage to change the things I can, and wisdom to know the difference." These and other similar prayers often bring a sense of spiritual well being and peace.

Besides formal prayers, we can talk to God informally. Swedenborg defines prayer as "conversation with God." Just try talking to him. Initially, you might feel silly, seemingly talking to no one. But that changes because you begin to recognize that you are not alone. God is with you to comfort and help you. God gives answers when you need them. They are not extraordinary signs and wonders but gifts of hope and understanding that come from a gentle voice within. Indeed, we recognize it as our own voice, but it does not express thoughts from our own minds. The voice comes from a higher power, from God. Listen to what Swedenborg has to say about this, as found in *Arcana Coelestia* ¶2535:

> *Regarded in itself prayer is talking to God and at the same time some inner view of the things that are being prayed for. Answering to this there is something akin to an influx into the perception or thought of the person's mind, which brings about a certain opening of the interiors towards God. But the experience varies according to the person's state and according to the essence of whatever he is praying for. If the prayer springs from love and faith, and if they are wholly celestial and spiritual things about which and for which he prays, something like a revelation is present within the prayer, which manifests itself in the feelings of the one praying in the form of hope, comfort, or some inward joy.*

In order to receive that perception of the divine presence with the hope and joy, we need not only to talk but to listen. We learn not to talk *at* God, but *with* God. It is easy to fall into the habit of yakking at God, never stopping long enough to listen for an answer. Have you found yourself in a conversation with someone who talks nonstop so that you can't get a word in edgewise? Perhaps that's how God feels when we pray to him but never give him a chance to reply. Providing the opening that lets God's response slip into our consciousness is the role of meditation.

MEDITATION

Meditation trains us to become better listeners. In meditation we clear our minds of the day's problems; we relax and open our spiritual windows and doors to let the light shine in. There are many ways to meditate, but, in general, meditation is learning how to relax our whole being, to be quiet, and to listen—to listen within.

The biblical story of Elijah is familiar. He hid from Jezebel who sent her armies to kill him. He was surely in need of God. An angel of the Lord led him from the cave where he was hiding to show him in a dramatic way that God was still with him. He showed him the wind ripping through rocks, but God was not in the wind. The angel showed Elijah a great earthquake, but God was not in the earthquake. He showed him a raging fire, but God was not in the fire. Then Elijah heard a still small voice. Within that voice was his Creator.

Often we look for a great sign of God's presence in our lives. We look for miracle cures outside ourselves: self-help books, philosophies, religions. All of these can help us to understand God, but they can't make us perceive him. We wait anxiously for one great truth to zoom from the sky and crush all our problems, for a thundering revelation to show us the way, or for an overwhelming sensation of love that will lift us into God's arms. But we won't find God in these things either. God is not in the wind, the earthquake, or the fire. We simply need to stop running, talking, and searching; we need to begin listening. God is the still small voice within that gently speaks to us all of the time if only we listen.

Think about this. When a child is lost in the woods, the child often begins a frantic search to find the lost path. Often panicking, the child runs blindly, only to enter a deeper state of panic and confusion, and gets farther off from the original place. That is why children are taught, "Stay where you are if you get lost. Someone will find you." This applies to adults as well. I knew a man who was lost on a hunting expedition and spent an entire night in below-zero temperatures walking around and around a tree until the search party found him. This was prudent action, but he found it hard to keep his panic down. He really wanted to run and shout, but knew he might hurt himself in the darkness.

It is the same in our search for God. We feel alone, lost, and confused. Our natural reaction is to keep running, trying one path or another to find him. Instead, stop, wait, and listen. God is there—he has always been there and he always knows where we are—ready to comfort and help. But we must open our eyes and our hearts and accept his help and warm embrace. Through meditation, we learn to be still, to recognize and accept our God.

CONSCIOUS CONTACT

The eleventh step tells us that "through prayer and meditation we improve our conscious contact with God. . . ." It is a conscious contact because, by working these steps. we come not only to know *of* him, we also come to *know* him. We not only love God, but we also feel that love. We seek and find him in our daily routines. It is a perceptible contact with God, at times astonishingly so.

My friend Glenn tells a story that offers a good close to this chapter. It was a Friday afternoon, the day before Glenn's wedding. It was imperative that he get to the bank before it closed; he needed to make a sizable withdrawal for his honeymoon. Work was hectic that day, leaving him only fifteen minutes to get to the bank—across town. En route, he encountered one red light after another, and then found himself in a traffic jam with about seven minutes left before the bank closed. However, he didn't pray for green lights or less traffic or that the bank would still be open. He simply prayed, "Please, God, let everything work out all right." Arriving at the bank twenty minutes late, he went to the drive-in window where the teller was closing for the day. He briefly told her his plight. She was sympathetic; she opened the window and gave him his money. Driving home he joyously reflected on his prayers and thanked God for making "everything work out." In this moment of elation, he looked up to heaven and shouted "Yahoo!" As his eyes focused back to his driving, he was stunned to read the license plate on the car in front of him: "Yahoo 2."

EXERCISES FOR STEP ELEVEN

Learning to pray and to meditate

1. In a stressful time, try reciting the Serenity Prayer: "God, grant me the serenity to accept the things I cannot change, courage to change the things I can, and wisdom to know the difference." See if it makes a difference.

2. In a state of fear or loss of control over destructive tendencies, recite the Lord's Prayer. Imagine that you are saying it, hand in hand, with eleven other people who are praying for your deliverance. Notice any change in your perception of the problem.

3. Each morning when you awake, say a prayer asking God to show you his will and to give you the power to carry it out. See if your days begin to change.

Step Twelve

Having had a spiritual awakening as the result of these steps, we tried to carry this message to others and to practice these principles in all our affairs.

IF YOU REFLECT on all the processes that have taken place within you as you have worked these steps, you will recognize what an incredible journey you have taken. When beginning this journey, you recognized your lack of power over destructive tendencies; it was not a comforting time. Sometimes these tendencies drove you to think or do things that hurt you and others. Even when recognizing that these destructive forces were real, you did not have the power to change, though you wanted to. Impulsively, bad feelings within you emerged from time to time: fear, guilt, anger, lust, want. These ruled your life.

As you began to work these steps and could acknowledge from the heart that you were degraded spiritually but could not raise yourself up, an open hand appeared, reaching out to give help. Within that painful recognition of your own powerlessness, there appeared an embryo of hope. Perhaps there was a way out; perhaps there was a power greater than yourself that could save you.

At first it was difficult to believe in such a power and to turn your will and your life over to his care. With no other solution, however, you tried with all your might to trust in this mysterious being, to let go and let God. It was a long up-and-down process. Some days you felt so much in his care that you thought you could walk on water if you believed strongly enough. On other days, the destructive inner voices and doubts became so powerful and so persuasive that you found yourself sinking back into bad thought patterns and old habits. Yet you recognized that every time you cried out to this higher power he was there to take you into his arms and rescue you from the spiritual storms that encompassed you.

After working the program, you began to feel much better about yourself and your life; nevertheless, you still felt you were wandering in the haze at times. You knew you had destructive tendencies within you, but it was difficult to define them clearly. You had problems, but they seemed so many—so intertwined and meshed together—that it was impossible to solve them one at a time.

With a new trust in God and a sense of his awesome power, you began to take a personal inventory to discover the nature of your wrongs. By discovering these deeper destructive forces within you and confessing them before God, yourself, and others, they became defined, almost tangible, and you were able to deal with them.

You began a course of action to rid yourself of these destructive tendencies and character defects. One by one you turned them over to God. One by one they began to lose their power as this greater power took charge within your life, ordering your life, removing the destructive and disorderly, and replacing them with goodness, peace of mind, joy, and love. You went forward on your spiritual journey with ease, correcting the mistakes of the past, focusing on the vast potential for good in your life. Certainly there were times when you tripped and stumbled. There were times, too, when you wandered off the path and maybe went backward for a while. But now you had the compass to find the right path again and to stay on it. Through regular self-examination, through prayer and meditation, and through a useful and productive life, you moved farther and farther down the road toward spiritual success. Every step of that path filled your whole being with true happiness and a heartfelt union with your God.

A SPIRITUAL AWAKENING

If you haven't yet had any of these rewarding experiences, be patient; you will if you follow these steps. As we go through this process, something happens; we have a "spiritual awakening." It is not a sudden and miraculous change in our lives; we don't awaken as a completely new, perfect, and wonderful person. We do not have angelic visions or become endowed with special psychic powers. We simply find that we have awakened spiritually. We begin to see and understand ourselves, our lives, our God, and our neighbor in a clearer light. We realize we have risen out of the darkness of moral apathy and spiritual neglect into the light of pure and living truth.

The move from dark to light is how many people describe their spiritual journey. It is like coming out of the darkness into the light or being blind to life but now suddenly seeing life in perspective. It is waking up from a nightmare to a bright reality. These awakenings may last only a few moments, or we may seem to wake up to a new world and never go back into the same sleep. These spiritual awakenings do occur when you work the twelve steps.

The experience of spiritual awakening is different with each person. With some it is a sudden realization of the changes that have taken place in their spiritual lives. One man told me that he awoke in the middle of the night to get a drink of water. As he passed the bathroom mirror, he noticed something different. He looked again into the mirror and realized he was staring at a different person. It was the same body but a different character. He wasn't staring at the guilt-ridden, fearful person he once was. He wasn't staring at the careless, irresponsible man he had struggled with for so long. He was looking at a loving, caring, thoughtful person who felt great about himself and life. You see, these spiritual awakenings can hit you anywhere, even in the bathroom in the middle of the night.

With others, spiritual awakening is a growing awareness of life and its meaning. One person described it by saying, "I had no sudden awakening. I just began to realize more and more that I had a purpose in life, that God was caring for me, and that I had big responsibilities too. It was as if I had been dreaming a boring dream—work, dinner, television, bed—day after day. But one day the dream ended. I was awake! I was alive! I could feel life for the first time. I cared. I loved. I felt cared for, for the first time."

With some, spiritual awakening comes in the form of perceiving the existence of God in their lives. They realize that God is not off somewhere sitting on a throne, indifferent toward themselves and the human race. They recognize that God is everywhere—in nature, in the beauty of every flower, tree and field, in the stars, in the heavens, in the face and eyes of others, even within their very being.

These are a few examples of the kinds of spiritual awakenings that come from following the twelve steps. The variety in these experiences is unending, and no two are exactly alike. But all are real and meaningful.

CARRYING THE MESSAGE

This spiritual awakening quite naturally leads to the second part of step twelve—telling other people about the program. The alcoholic tells other alcoholics about AA; the overeater tells other overeaters about OA. Likewise, this twelve-step philosophy is for everyone. It is not merely a way to recruit and thus perpetuate the spiritual program. Far from it. We carry this message to others because it is not only charitable to do so, but it also helps us as individuals to continue to grow in our own spiritual program.

Obviously, if we really are becoming spiritual people who sincerely care about others, we are going to want to share what we know with the hope that the program will also help them. If, having worked these steps and had a spiritual awakening, we decide not to let others know about it, something in our spiritual development has gone wrong. We have freely received; we must freely give. We have learned; we must teach. We have been healed; it is our turn to cooperate with the higher power to bring healing to others. If we have been working the program, we will want to do these things; and, as we share these wonderful insights and experiences, we will continue to grow.

When we give of ourselves—lending a hand, sharing an insight, introducing someone to the basic teachings of this program—we also receive. The love and friendships that develop by our giving are deep, spiritual, and lasting. We raise our sense of self-worth as we see how God works through us to lead others to a better path and a fulfilling relationship with him. When we teach others, we, in turn, learn much more about the program, about ourselves, about life. Any teacher can tell you that he or she learns more by teaching a subject than by studying it,

I attest to this by sharing a personal experience. I had been involved in a twelve-step group for five years and thought I knew much about the program and my own spiritual life. Yet, when I began to speak to groups about this program, to study and reflect on the various aspects of each of the steps for writing this book and others, I found a treasure full of new knowledge and understanding. I learned much more about this program in one year of studying, teaching, and helping others than in the previous five years of actively working the program for myself. Moreover, I didn't learn just universal truths that would be of use to other people, but I learned more truths about my own life and spiritual development.

It is not merely a matter of the intellect. We are not simply blessed with greater knowledge and insight by sharing this philosophy; we also learn love.

One of the most touching experiences of my life came in a very unusual place. I was in Chicago to speak at a half-way house for alcoholics and drug users. This was not your ordinary half-way house. The inhabitants were "skid row" in every sense of the term. They were homeless, hardened, promiscuous, and addicted. Some sold their bodies to get their fix; some sold drugs, thereby spreading the horror of their lives to others. In fact, when I came to the place, an escort met me at the door and guided me, for my own safety, through the building. I waited in a small room with a couch and a chair until the group gathered for my speech. I was thinking, "What on earth have I gotten into? These people don't want to hear about God, or love, or finding another way!" Panic swept over me as I walked toward the assembly room to face this crowd. Since I had no time to change my speech, I began by talking about our powerlessness, about God, about hitting the wall of illusion. I spoke at length about Peter walking on the water to meet the Lord.

What an experience! I have never spoken to a more receptive, accepting, willing audience—and I have had many audiences. They drank in every word; they nodded their approval, smiled, laughed, applauded. I felt like a messenger of light appearing before publicans and sinners of old, bringing good news of a new way and a new life. I felt *honored* to be in their presence. I knew then that we all are really God's children—even those who have gone astray—and that it's never too late to turn back. If they were willing to try, God would work with them. He would feed them with spiritual knowledge and lead them like a shepherd. God would lift them out of their turmoil and confusion. I felt a degree of the love that God has for these people; I played a small part in helping God to help them. These new feelings and insights—a spiritual experience—would not have happened had I not been there to share the message of this program. It was a simple thing, yet it was so rewarding. When we help to heal another, we, too, are healed. It is an amazing process.

A close acquaintance strengthened this point for me with the story of a painful episode that involved hitting the wall of illusion, coming back to his senses, working the program, and finally being healed by completing this twelfth step. He had fallen for the grand illusion that having an affair would bring happiness. To make a long story short, he had an affair, and he hit the wall hard when it became generally known. He lost his spouse, family life, even his job. He had to live with those external conditions; but the guilt, the pain, and the insanity of it all haunted him for years.

By working this twelve-step program, my friend slowly came to terms with himself and with God. It was a long, slow process. The initial anguish had subsided, but he still felt pain when he reflected on it. Not until he took the twelfth step was he freed from the bonds of his infidelity.

Actually, this step was thrust upon him. A good friend was heading down the same path he had taken two years earlier. The friend wanted to know if an affair was worth a "dual life." Without hesitation, my friend sounded a loud warning, making a desperate effort to stop the man from making this mistake. He cited every personal painful memory, hoping to change his mind. He called the friend on the phone to talk it over in more detail and to offer help with the challenge.

After that phone call, my friend said that saw his own affair as it really was. Every illusion disappeared. His false ideas were exposed and the lies he had told himself during the affair emerged and were cut in two. He said, "It was like a light shining from God that lit up my entire being. I understood the affair for what it really was, how and why I was wrong. I was truly sorry and knew for the first time that I was forgiven." In his efforts to stop another from spiritual harm, he himself had been healed.

If it can work for someone who has gone through such personal hell, it can work for all. Each of us hits the wall now and then, some harder than others, and feels the self-inflicted wounds of our personal transgressions. Yet we can become wounded healers, and in healing others, we will find our own healing.

Unquestionably, when we give we receive so much more in return. We become human beings in the image and likeness of our Maker, full of his love and wisdom. This radiates from our being, touching and enriching every life that comes in contact with our own. Step twelve brings all to fruition. The work of this program and the struggle to order our lives give us the ability to help other people order their own lives. In our lives for others, we begin the work that God has accomplished spiritually within us. We are there to give comfort and hope, to offer strength, to teach, to lead, to guide.

PRACTICING THESE PRINCIPLES

This twelve-step program creates a process for achieving happiness and spirituality. To be of help, these steps must be used in daily life. Merely knowing them will not bring about spiritual growth; doing them will. Many people in different twelve-step programs talk about the steps but don't really practice them; consequently, they do not grow spiritually. They become like broken records, recounting the same problems over and over at every twelve-step meeting yet seemingly unable to see the relation between the various steps and their own lives. This is sad.

These steps work for those who work them. As a person incorporates these steps into his or her daily life, the path to deeper spirituality becomes more clear, progress is made, and happiness becomes a condition of life. Work the steps! Work them often! Work them diligently!

What results from practicing these principles in daily life? We experience a spiritual awakening, true, but we also look at our past and compare it with the present. We realize we are no longer powerless. Whereas our destructive tendencies once ruled our lives with a tyranny, today we are the masters of our own destinies. Our spiritual part reigns over all the lower regions. With this new higher power as our source of support, we feel a sense of total freedom, full self-determination, and well-being. We are genuinely happy for the first time in our lives. And these new feelings get better every day.

EXERCISES FOR STEP TWELVE

Seeing progress; carrying the message

1. Reflect. Have you had a spiritual awakening? What evidence points to it?

2. Tell someone about this program.

How to Use This Book

ANY INDIVIDUAL WILL benefit from reading this book and practicing the exercises. However, I strongly recommend that you follow this program with at least one other person or an entire group. Others have accomplished this in the past by asking friends or their spouse to read the book and work through the program together. Some have put a small advertisement in the local paper to invite interested people to join a study/spiritual-support group based on the book.

One chapter a week is read and one of the exercises at the end of the chapter is assigned and reported on the following week. The program lasts for twelve weeks but can be repeated by assigning different tasks and simply going around the room for a "spiritual check-in."

Practicing this program with others offers support. Spiritual growth doesn't happen by reading any book; it happens by taking steps to change your life and finding support for making those changes. By reporting on your progress to others, you concentrate more fully on the exercises, and ideas and experiences are shared. Besides, fellowships based on spiritual growth are truly special and may last throughout your life.

A GUIDE FOR A FELLOWSHIP PROGRAM

Anyone can lead a support group for this book by using the following guide:

Opening welcome
Welcome to this twelve-step fellowship for spiritual growth. We will begin this session with a brief review of the rules, "How It Works," and share our experiences of the last session's exercises.

These twelve steps work for those who work them. They are a guide to progress in all areas of life. We, like other twelve-step fellowships, claim spiritual progress rather than spiritual perfection. To the degree that we are willing to work these steps, we will find true sanity, happiness, and spirituality in our lives.

And remember, although we are not anonymous, what individuals say here should stay here.

Rules Reminder

As we take turns, be considerate of others in the length of time you speak. Remember, everything said here should stay here. No one has to talk; you may pass. This is a self-supported group, and we will pass the basket each week to cover some of our costs. Feel free to contribute or not to contribute.

How it Works*

This fellowship is not a substitute for AA or Al-Anon or other programs dealing with specific addictions, but it can act as a supplement to these. This is a twelve-step program for everyone, from every background, who desires to grow spiritually. Here we share our joys and our sorrows as we search for wholeness and spirituality in our lives.

Here are the steps suggested as a program for spirituality:

1. We admitted that we were powerless over our destructive tendencies and that, when we followed them, our lives became unmanageable.

2. Came to believe that a power greater than ourselves could bring us true sanity.

3. Made a decision to turn our will and our lives over to the care of God, as we understood him.

4. Made a searching and fearless moral inventory of ourselves.

---

*To be read by a member of the group.

5. Admitted to God, to ourselves, and to another human being the exact nature of our wrongs.

6. Became entirely ready to have God remove all these defects of character.

7. Humbly asked God to remove our shortcomings and began a new life.

8. Made a list of all the persons we had harmed and became willing to make amends to all.

9. Began to make amends, to do good, to be honest and faithful in all our affairs, and to walk humbly with our God.

10. Continued to take personal inventory and when we were wrong promptly admitted it.

11. Sought through prayer and meditation to improve our conscious contact with God, as we understood him, praying only for knowledge of his will for us and the power to carry that out.

12. Having had a spiritual awakening as the result of these steps, we tried to carry this message to others and to practice these principles in all our affairs.

Review of exercise
Review the exercises that were assigned in the previous session. Going around the room, each person tells what he or she has learned from performing the exercise chosen. (Exercises can be found at the end of each chapter.)

Reading from the book
A volunteer reads selections from this book, dealing with the particular step the group is working on for that session.

The lesson learned
Going around the room, each person briefly discusses what he or she learned from the reading, or any new insights, and how it might apply to his or her particular situation.

Assignment

Review the exercises assigned for the next session. Remind the group members to be ready at the next session to report on their experiences of practicing these exercises.

Closing

The Lord's Prayer

Bibliography

Al-Anon's Twelve Steps and Twelve Traditions. New York: Al-Anon Family Group Headquarters, Inc., 1981.

Alcoholics Anonymous (Big Book). New York: Alcoholics Anonymous World Services, 1939, 1955, 1976.

Beattie, Melody. *Codependent No More: How to Stop Controlling Others and Start Caring for Yourself.* New York: Harper–Hazelden, 1987.

Bittner, Vernon J. *You Can Help With Your Healing.* Minneapolis, Minnesota: Augsburg Publishing House, 1979.

Came To Believe. New York: Alcoholics Anonymous World Services, 1973.

Klass, Joe. *The Twelve Steps to Happiness.* Center City, Minnesota: Hazelden Educational Materials, 1982.

Narcotics Anonymous. Van Nuys, California: Narcotics Anonymous World Service Office, 1982.
Rhodes, Peter S. *Aim.* Bryn Athyn, Pennsylvania: self-published, 1991.

_____. *Aim: The Workbook.* San Francisco: J. Appleseed: 1995.

Schnarr, Grant. *Return to the Promised Land: The Story of Our Spiritual Recovery.* West Chester, Pennsylvania: Swedenborg Foundation, 1997.

Swedenborg, Emanuel. *Arcana Caelestia.* 12 vols. Tr. John Elliott. London: Swedenborg Society, 1983–1998.

_____. *Arcana Coelestia.* 12 vols. Tr. J. Clowes. Rvd. and ed. J. F. Potts. 2nd ed. West Chester, Pennsylvania: Swedenborg Foundation, 1995–1998.

————. *Charity: The Practice of Neighborliness.* Tr. W. F. Wunsch. Rvd. and ed. W. R. Woofenden. 2nd ed. West Chester, Pennsylvania: Swedenborg Foundation, 1995.

————. *Divine Love and Wisdom.* Tr. J. C. Ager. 2nd ed. West Chester, Pennsylvania: Swedenborg Foundation, 1995.

————. *Divine Providence.* Tr. W. F. Wunsch. 2nd ed. West Chester, Pennsylvania: Swedenborg Foundation, 1996.

————. *Four Doctrines.* Tr. J. F. Potts. 2nd ed. West Chester, Pennsylvania: Swedenborg Foundation, 1997.

————. *True Christian Religion.* 2 vols. Tr. J. C. Ager. 2nd ed. West Chester, Pennsylvania: Swedenborg Foundation, 1996

The Twelve Steps: A Healing Journey. Center City, Minnesota: Hazelden Foundation, 1986.

The Twelve Steps for Everyone . . . Who Really Wants Them. Minneapolis, Minnesota: CompCare Publishers, 1975.

Twelve Steps and Twelve Traditions. New York: Alcoholics Anonymous World Services, 1952.

Whitfield, Charles L. *Co-dependence: Healing the Human Condition.* Deerfield Beach, Florida: Health Communications, Inc., 1991.

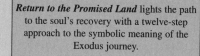

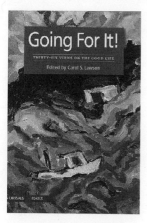